PENGUIN

THE ECLOGUES

ADVISORY EDITOR: BETTY RADICE

Publius Vergilius Maro was born in 70 BC near Mantua in Cisalpine Gaul, the north of Italy, where his parents owned a farm. He had a good education and went to perfect it in Rome. There he came under the influence of Epicureanism and later joined an Epicurean colony on the Gulf of Naples where he was based for the rest of his life. In 42 BC he began to write the *Eclogues*, which he completed in 37 BC, the year in which he accompanied Horace to Brindisi. The *Georgics* were finished in 29 BC, and he devoted the rest of his life to the composition of the *Aeneid*. In his last year he started on a journey to Greece; he fell ill at Megara and returned to Italy, but he died in 19 BC on reaching Brindisi.

•

Arthur Guy Lee was born in 1918 and educated at the Glebe House, Hunstanton, Loretto School, Musselburgh and St John's College, Cambridge, where he was admitted a Fellow in 1946; he has served the College successively as Tutor, Praelector and Librarian, and the University as Lecturer in Classics. His publications include commentaries on Ovid's *Metamorphoses* I and Cicero's *Stoic Paradoxes*, poems in Latin and English, and verse translations of Ovid's *Amores* and Tibullus's *Elegies*.

VIRGIL

THE ECLOGUES

THE LATIN TEXT WITH A

VERSE TRANSLATION AND BRIEF NOTES

BY GUY LEE

PENGUIN BOOKS

Penguin Books Ltd, Harmondsworth, Middlesex, England
Viking Penguin Inc., 40 West 23rd Street, New York, New York 10010, U.S.A.
Penguin Books Australia Ltd, Ringwood, Victoria, Australia
Penguin Books Canada Limited, 2801 John Street, Markham, Ontario, Canada L3R 1B4
Penguin Books (N.Z.) Ltd, 182–190 Wairau Road, Auckland 10, New Zealand

First published by Francis Cairns (School of Classics,
Abercromby Square, University of Liverpool, P.O Box 147,
Liverpool L69 3BX, Great Britain) as Liverpool Latin Texts I 1980
Revised edition published in Penguin Books 1984
Reprinted 1987

Printed and bound in Great Britain by
Cox & Wyman Ltd, Reading
Filmset in Monophoto Ehrhardt by
Northumberland Press Ltd, Gateshead

FOR KENNETH McLEISH

CONTENTS

ACKNOWLEDGEMENTS

The translator wishes to record his thanks: to Kenneth McLeish and Wendell Clausen for encouragement, criticism and guidance, literary and scholarly; to Helen Lee and Patricia Huskinson for patient listening and many decisions; to Frederic Raphael and Theodore Redpath for valuable suggestions; to the Delegates of the Clarendon Press for permission to reprint the Latin text of the *Eclogues* established in 1969 by Sir Roger Mynors, departures from which (including punctuation) are noted at *Eclogues* II.7, III.79 and 102, X. 5, 71 and 72; to the Editor of *Thames Poetry* for permission to reprint the translations of *Eclogues* II and X; and finally to Francis Cairns for his kindness in undertaking publication of the first edition.

He has consulted various commentaries, notably Servius, La Cerda, Ruaeus, Martyn, Conington, Page, Coleman and Williams; in addition he has had the advantage of Wendell Clausen's typescript notes to *Eclogues* I, II, VII, VIII and IX.

He has also consulted the translations of B. H. Kennedy, Royds, Mackail, Fairclough, Valéry, Rieu, Day Lewis, Putnam, Berg, Sisson, Boyle and Alpers. Identical phrase does not necessarily imply indebtedness: for instance, though the rendering of *Eclogue* X.56–7 was adapted from Rieu, that of X.47–8 was not; translators often hit on the same form of words independently.

For this second edition the introduction has been much enlarged, each *Eclogue* given an introductory note, and the translation and notes revised. The translator is deeply indebted to the scholarship of Wendell Clausen (once again) and of Patrick Wilkinson, who read the first edition and the first draft of the additional material with great care and suggested many improvements. He again owes special thanks for shrewd criticism to Helen Lee and to Patricia Huskinson, who also did the typing. The main revisions to the translation occur at the following places: *Eclogue* I.3–4, 67–9, 77; II.69; III.14, 52, 74; IV.50; VII. 32; VIII.97–9; IX.32, 66–7.

INTRODUCTION

'Not another translation of the *Eclogues*?' the knowledgeable reader may protest, remembering that there have already been at least seven published in English since 1949. True, but of these seven only one – that of A. J. Boyle (1976) – has attempted to reproduce as closely as possible in English verse what Virgil's Latin actually says. Boyle's success is remarkable and sets a new standard for translators of Latin poetry, but some may feel that his versification, based as it is on 'a five or six stress line of eleven to fifteen syllables', despite its similarity in syllabic variation to the Virgilian hexameter of thirteen to seventeen syllables, is nevertheless not regular enough; for every Virgilian line, as the name 'hexameter' implies, contains precisely six metrical stresses, and not five or six. In other words, Virgil's versification is strict, not free, and a modern translator may well decide that an important part of his task, despite prevailing fashion in contemporary poetry, is to reproduce that regularity in his English version. This the present translator has attempted to do, choosing as his medium the English Alexandrine.

The critic will of course object that Virgil's line is dactylic, whereas the Alexandrine is iambic, and that by adopting the iambic rhythm the translator plays false to his original. To this objection the following answer can be made: first, that in English poetry blank verse (iambic rhythm) is the commonest medium, just as the dactylic hexameter is in Latin; secondly, that in practice the English dactylic hexameter offers more syllables than are normally needed to render its Latin equivalent, whereas the blank verse line contains too few. These considerations point to the Alexandrine, or twelve syllable iambic line, as the natural representative in English of the Latin hexameter, provided that a feminine ending and certain substitutions be occasionally allowed in order to increase the number of syllables available, and conversely that now and then a trochaic line be admissible.

So much for metre; now diction. To the best of our guessing Virgil's Latin in the *Eclogues*, particularly in the non-dialogue ones, is quite often far removed from ordinary Latin speech. This characteristic must be represented in a translation, if it is to be faithful and not self-indulgent or trendy, however vividly so. Occasionally Virgil uses an archaism. The clearest example is *cuium* for *cuius* in the first line of *Eclogue* III, which was parodied in the poet's lifetime and is hard to represent in English; the best solution to present itself was 'Meliboeus his' for 'Meliboeus's' in that same line, on the analogy of 'Achilles his armour' in Sir Thomas Browne. *Tegmine* in the opening line of the collection was also parodied, and again sets the translator a difficult problem; at all events the English line must have a certain strangeness, not to say awkwardness, about it. Poetry is often the unfamiliar, the different, the mysterious, even the slightly odd. *Phaëthontiades* is a very odd word in Latin and must therefore, it can be argued, appear in the English too and not be paraphrased into 'Phaëthon's sisters', for the word does not 'mean' that; it is a way of referring or alluding to Phaëthon's sisters and means itself.

Virgil's contemporary and friend the poet Horace characterized the verse of the *Eclogues* as *molle atque facetum*. Fortunately it is possible to demonstrate with some precision what he meant by these two adjectives. For Cicero, writing only a few years before Horace, refers in his *Tusculan Disputations* to *facetum illud Bionis*, 'that — remark of Bion's'. Now Bion, a Greek philosopher of the third century BC, commenting on a line of the *Iliad* where it is said of Agamemnon in difficulties 'Many the hairs of his head he tore out by the roots,' remarked: 'He must have thought baldness would relieve his depression.' Secondly, in his *De Finibus* Cicero makes his brother Quintus describe the poetry (*carmen*) at the beginning of Sophocles' *Oedipus Coloneus* as *mollissimum*. Literally translated the lines in question read as follows (the blind Oedipus is addressing the daughter who has accompanied him into exile on the discovery that he was unwittingly guilty of murdering his father and marrying his mother):

> Child of a blind old man, Antigone,
> What country have we reached or what men's town?
> Who will today give welcome to the vagrant
> Oedipus with meagre charities?
> Requesting little and receiving less,
> I make do even with that.
> For suffering and time's long company
> And, thirdly, breeding teach me tolerance.
> But oh, child, if you see a resting-place
> In some grove, whether secular or sacred,
> Halt there and sit me down, that we may ask
> Our whereabouts; for we have come to learn,
> Strangers from locals, and to do as we are told.

With the help of these two pointers from Cicero perhaps we shall not be too far astray if we render Horace's *molle atque facetum* as 'sensitive and witty', or even 'sensitive and ironic'.[1]

Clearly the translator of Virgil's pastoral poetry must bear

1. Some hundred and thirty years (about AD 95) after the publication of Horace *Satires* I, Quintilian in his great work *On the Education of the Orator* VI. 3.19–20 writes: 'Again, I am of opinion that the word *facetum* is not applicable solely to what raises a laugh. For if it were, Horace would not have said that nature had granted Virgil a *facetum* kind of poetry. I think the term more probably refers to a rightness and a certain cultivated elegance.' He then cites in support a quotation which our MSS present in a slightly garbled form: it includes the words *pedes faceti* but it is not clear whether these are metrical 'feet'. However, it *is* clear that Quintilian wants to give the word in the Horatian context a meaning which it does not normally have. I suspect that his unconscious reason was the almost religious veneration in which Virgil was then held, as Rome's greatest poet, the author of her national epic the *Aeneid*. For the more generally accepted view, which supports Quintilian's interpretation, see Wilkinson (1969), pp. 21–2.

Horace's words in mind, even though he knows that his best can never equal the original, for there can only be one of those. This last proposition (obvious, but seldom fully realized) carries the corollary that a translation of poetry is open to objection at virtually any point; it can always be criticized for not being the original. My aim therefore is the modest one of giving the reader a metrical version in which he will be able to recognize every word of Virgil's Latin. There is a pleasure in such recognition and even those readers who know no Latin at all will usually be able to follow, should they so wish, the Latin from the English (indeed, one could teach oneself Latin in this way).

Pastoral, or, to be more precise, bucolic poetry was invented by the Syracusan Greek Theocritus round about 275 BC. The two words derive respectively from Latin *pastor* ('feeder, shepherd') and Greek *boukolos* ('cowman'). Theocritus may have got the idea partly from the mimes (in Doric prose) of his fifth-century compatriot Sophron, partly from the actual practice of Sicilian shepherds (who will surely have played pipes and sung songs during the long hours of watching their flocks[2]), but perhaps even more from enjoyment of the countryside on the island of Cos, of which he writes from detailed personal knowledge in *Idyll* VII, and whose flora has been shown to agree with that of his poems.[3] They are commonly known as *Idylls* (*eidyllia*), which may mean 'little pictures' or 'little pieces', but there is no evidence that this title goes back to the poet himself.[4] Paradoxically, he writes them in a refined form of the Homeric hexameter but in the Doric dialect, a combination of local accent

2. At *Iliad* 18.525 Homer mentions herdsmen piping as they follow their herds, and I have seen Romanian shepherds piping in a TV documentary.

3. See Lindsell (1937), pp. 83–91.

4. Similarly *Eclogues* (*Eclogae*) was not Virgil's title, but came from the grammarians' habit of referring to *Piece* 1, *Piece* 2, etc., the meaning of the Greek word *ekloge* being 'extract, piece'. Later *Ecloga* acquired the bogus etymology *Aig-loga*, 'Goat-talk', whence came French *Églogue*, Italian *Egloga*, etc. Virgil called his collection *Bucolics* (*Bucolica*), because that was the title given to Theocritus's collection.

and epic metre which in itself, and quite apart from the pastoral subject-matter, must have been something new and surprising to his original readers.[5] These pastoral *Idylls*, which in fact amount to only about one third of his surviving work, range in tone from the earthy realism of IV and V (the latter the ancestor of the pastoral singing-match) through the dramatic irony, humour and pathos of XI (the Cyclops's song to Galatea, ancestor of the pastoral lover's complaint), to the nostalgic plangency of I (Thyrsis's lament for Daphnis, ancestor of the so-called 'pastoral elegy', of which Milton's *Lycidas* is the most famous English example). Indeed, Theocritean pastoral, despite its rustic language and form, is quite often poetry like *Lycidas* – learned, allusive and *cantabile*:

> *Kai tu didou tan aiga to te skuphos, hos ken amelxas*
> *Speiso tais Moisais. O khairete pollaki, Moisai,*
> *Khairet'. Ego d'ummin kai es husteron hadion aiso.*
>
> And you, give the goat and the bowl, that having milked
> I may pour to the Muses. O farewell many times, Muses,
> Farewell. I shall sing you sweeter still hereafter.

Thyrsis in *Idyll* I melodiously claims the rustic prize and ends his song about Daphnis as though it were a Homeric Hymn.

These qualities must have appealed to, indeed enthralled, the young Virgil when he first met the work of Theocritus more than two hundred years later, for he decided to attempt the naturalization of Theocritean pastoral in Latin, and in the process (which is likely to have been lengthy, as the *Eclogues* were not completed until he was over thirty) he too learnt to be learned, allusive and *cantabile*:

> *Et uitula tu dignus et hic, et quisquis amores*
> *aut metuet dulcis aut experietur amaros,*
> *claudite iam riuos, pueri; sat prata biberunt.*

5. See Griffin (1980), pp. 139–40. The Doric dialect had previously been used for choral lyric.

Both you and he have earned the heifer – so have all
Who fear the sweet or feel the bitterness of love.
Now close the sluices, lads; the fields have drunk their fill.

Palaemon gives musical judgement at the end of the singing-match in *Eclogue* III, with a paradoxical variation on the theme of bitter-sweet love (Sappho's coinage originally, it would seem) and a final line that can be interpreted both literally and metaphorically. The chiming of *amores/amaros* in lines 1–2 and the alliteration of *m* are obvious, not so obvious is the assonance of *tu di-* in line 1 with *dulci* in line 2; the echo in lines 2–3 of *aut* ... *aut* in *claudite* and the alliteration of *p* and *r* and the repetition of *ri* are obvious, not so obvious is *-rata biberunt* as partially reversing the vowel sounds of *-ietur amaros.*

But Virgil could not represent everything in Theocritus. What could he do about the Doric? There was no satisfactory equivalent in Latin and the few archaisms or rusticities of speech to be found in the *Eclogues* hardly make up for that deficiency; perhaps, though, the Theocritean surprise of combining Doric dialect and epic hexameter is represented by the Virgilian surprise of shepherds with bucolic Greek names uttering melodious Latin verses and sometimes alluding to contemporary Romans. Nor could Virgil exactly represent the Theocritean hexameter; the Latin language offered too few dactyls (–˘˘) to enable him faithfully to reproduce the two features characteristic of Theocritus's pastoral hexameter: bucolic diaeresis and third-foot, weak caesura. Diaeresis is a break between words which coincides with the end of a foot, and bucolic diaeresis is a break between words at the end of dactylic fourth foot, thus (*Eclogue* I.3):

nos patri-/ae fi-/nis et/dūlcĭă//linquimus/arua

This diaeresis occurs in almost every line of Theocritus, but far less often in Virgil (sixteen times in the eighty-three lines of *Eclogue* I); in compensation Virgil often allowed himself a spondaic diaeresis at the fourth foot, a thing which is rare in Theocritus, thus (*Eclogue* I.28):

candidi-|or post-|quam ton-|dēntī||barba ca-|debat

A caesura, on the other hand, is a break between words which occurs in the middle of a foot, and a weak caesura is such a break occurring after the first short syllable of a dactyl, thus (*Eclogue* I.5):

formo-|sam reso-|nārĕ||dŏ-|ces Ama-|ryllida|siluas

This third-foot, weak caesura occurs in at least 50 per cent of Theocritus's hexameters, but much less often in Virgil (fourteen times in the eighty-three lines of *Eclogue* I). Such, very briefly, are the important differences between the Virgilian and the Theocritean pastoral hexameters, differences virtually necessitated by the heavier, more spondaic character of the Latin language.

In Virgil's hands the *Idyll* turned into something rather different from its Theocritean prototype, both in content and form. This can be seen most clearly from a comparison of *Eclogue* II with *Idyll* XI. In the *Idyll*, Polyphemus the Cyclops, gigantic one-eyed shepherd of Homer's *Odyssey*, serenades the sea-nymph Galatea; the idea of that cannibalistic monster being in love is ludicrous, to say the least, but Theocritus's wit and humour make the paradox amusingly credible and even a touch pathetic (*Idyll* XI.54–63):

Alas that mother didn't give me gills!
I could dive down to you and kiss your hand
(If you refuse your mouth) and bring you either
White lilies or soft poppies with scarlet smackers –[6]
One blooms in summer, though, and one in winter,
So I couldn't bring you all these at one time.

6. 'Smackers': apparently poppy-petals were used in a form of *She loves me, she loves me not* where the lover laid the petal on his forearm and slapped it. The details are obscure: see Gow on Theocritus, *Idyll* III.29.

Dear mite, I'll learn to swim – now, yes, right now.
If a stranger comes here sailing in a ship –
I'll find out why you like life in the deep.

Theocritus takes a paradoxical subject from the world of myth and treats it naturalistically. Virgil takes a subject from real life and treats it romantically, playing down the humour, stressing the pathos and the poetry. Corydon, head-shepherd on a sheep-farm in Sicily, is a real person, a sensitive like the poet himself; indeed antiquity interpreted this poem as autobiography. The misunderstanding rests on the reader's subconscious feeling that the *Eclogues* hint at much that is autobiographical – a feeling he does not have when reading the pastoral *Idylls*, for Theocritus distances himself from his shepherds. In one exceptional *Idyll* (VII), however, the young man Simichidas is almost certainly the poet himself and the goatherd Lycidas probably an established poet of the time. Encouraged no doubt by this Theocritean precedent, Virgil goes further. On two occasions he openly invites the reader to identify him with a shepherd: in *Eclogue* VI Apollo addresses the poet as Tityrus and calls him a shepherd, while at the end of *Eclogue* V Menalcas claims to be author of *Eclogues* II and III; and this raises the question whether the Menalcas of *Eclogue* IX and the Tityrus of *Eclogue* I are not also Virgil. Can one wonder that antiquity looked to the *Eclogues* for information about his life?

The best *Life of Virgil* to come down to us (in three MSS of the ninth and tenth centuries) probably derives in large part from Suetonius, the early-second-century biographer, who will have had access to at least some reliable sources, including the written evidence of close friends of the poet.[7] In its present form this *Life* is ascribed to Donatus – probably Aelius Donatus, the fourth-century scholar whose most distinguished pupil was the future St Jerome. There are other and later *Lives* and fragments of information to be found elsewhere. Together all this amounts

7. See Gellius, *Noctes Atticae*, XVII.10.2.

to quite a sizeable 'tradition', but the task of sifting its truth from its falsehood is hard and controversial. It will be enough to give here the few generally agreed facts of his life until the composition of his *Eclogues*, and also some traditional personal details. He was born on 15 October 70 BC near Mantua in the Roman province of Cisalpine Gaul. He received the best education available, at Cremona, Milan and Rome, an indication that his father was a man of some substance. Thereafter he joined an Epicurean group at Naples, to study this philosophy, which he will probably have first met through reading Lucretius. There is a story that he appeared once as a barrister and decided that the law was not his line. The tradition reports him as a large man, tall and dark, of peasant appearance (if that is a fair translation of *facie rusticana* – alternatively, 'looking like a farmer'), very slow-spoken, almost like an illiterate (*paene indocto similem* – alternatively, 'you'd think he might have had no education'), shy and shunning publicity, bisexual, of weak health, and very abstemious. Apparently, his reading of poetry was totally compelling and could make even undistinguished lines sound good. Of his writing he used to say that he composed 'like a bear', referring to a popular belief that a bear's cubs were shapeless and sprawling at birth and had to be licked into shape and proportion by their mother: 'so his poetical brood at first looked rough and unfinished but by rehandling and working them over he gave them outlines of mouth and features (*or* expression)'.[8]

The *Eclogues* spring from the troubled times that followed the murder of Julius Caesar in March 44 BC, years when Italy was torn by civil war and the Mediterranean world split between contending Roman factions. *Eclogue* IV was written for the consulship of Gaius Asinius Pollio in 40 BC, after the Treaty of

8. Gellius, *Noctes Atticae*, XVII.10.2–3, and Pliny *Natural History* X.176. For a translation of Donatus's *Vita* see the Loeb edition of Suetonius, volume 2, pp. 465–83, or Camps (1969), Appendix 1; for a judicious discussion of the evidence see Wilkinson (1969), pp. 16–43.

Brindisi which, as Antony's representative, he had helped to bring about between Antony and Octavian (the future Augustus). This treaty, of which one important condition was that Antony should marry the sister of Octavian, at last gave promise of an enduring peace; no one at the time could know that the promise was soon to prove illusory. Virgil's pastoral world sometimes, especially in *Eclogues* I and IX, mirrors the disturbances of his real world, the Waste Land of the dying Roman Republic, to which Pollio refers in a letter to Cicero written in 43 BC after the carnage of the fighting round Mutina (Modena) – *uastitatem Italiae*, 'the desolation of Italy' (Cicero, *Ad Familiares* X.33.1). Other *Eclogues* are set in a countryside at peace, offering the reader a refreshing change from the life of the city.

It is, however, a commonly held belief that Virgil's *Eclogues* are set in Arcadia, 'the poet's golden land, where imagination found a refuge from the harsh prosaic life of the present' (to quote Conington, p.2), but like some other commonly held beliefs this turns out on investigation to be untrue. *Eclogue* I, with its mention of Tityrus's visit to Rome, appears to be set in Italy, II in Sicily, III, IV, V, VI and VIII in no named location, VII by the river Mincio in north Italy and IX (by inference from the mention of Mantua and Cremona) also in north Italy. In fact, the only *Eclogue* explicitly set in Arcadia is X, the last one.

But this conclusion, it will be argued, is all too literal-minded: Virgil's Arcadia must be understood in Conington's sense, metaphorically, as an imaginary world far removed from the trials and accidents of real life. But is that true? *Eclogue* I presents a countryside in turmoil and two farmers; one has been evicted and is on his way into exile, the other, an elderly ex-slave, has been more fortunate – authority has confirmed him in possession of a piece of fifth-rate land. In *Eclogue* II a head-shepherd (and therefore a man with time to stand back and feel sorry for himself) admits, against a background of agricultural labour, that he has had what might nowadays be called a nervous breakdown. In *Eclogue* III two shepherds meet and exchange insults, after which they decide on a singing-match and sing *inter alia* of wolves and gales, snakes in the grass, rams falling into rivers, sheep's milk drying up in hot weather, bulls losing weight after serving the cows, skinny lambs, and the evil eye. *Eclogue* IV sings of a Roman consul, refers to a crime committed by the Roman people, to a terror that grips the world and to a mysterious act of primeval treachery. In *Eclogue* V again two shepherds meet, the younger very touchy, and sing carefully balanced songs, one about the death of a mysterious shepherd named Daphnis, which caused a total failure of the harvest, the other about his ascension to heaven and worship as a god by the joyful country people. *Eclogue* VI does indeed transport us to an imaginary land where Silenus may be found asleep in a cave and where Fauns and wild beasts will dance to his singing, but some of the things he sings about can hardly be called Arcadian: Chaos, the Flood, theft, rape, bestiality, infanticide and cannibalism. In *Eclogue* VII a shepherd tells how two other shepherds, both Arcadians, met near Mantua for a singing-match, which he then reports: there is mention of envy, witchcraft, extremes of heat and cold, wolves, winter floods, summer drought and heavy rain. *Eclogue* VIII again transports us to an imaginary land where we hear the song of a man who ends by committing suicide and of a woman who practises black magic with apparent success. Finally *Eclogue* IX, and once more two shepherds, the elder of whom has been evicted from his farm and has lost his memory; there is talk about litigation and a narrow escape from murder thanks to a raven's timely croak from a hollow ilex.

The last paragraph has of course been slanted, for the reader's entertainment, by the citation of only those points that support the case and by their rhetorical sharpening. Proponents of the contrary view are equally selective in their choice of passage, and the truth, if it does not lie (unlucky homonym!) at the bottom of a well, lurks elusively somewhere in between the two points of view.[9] It cannot be denied that *Eclogue* X is set in Arcadia and that this *Eclogue* and at least two others (VI and VIII) take place in a world where the gods appear to mortals and where music has a magic power over nature. But that is not to say that the collection as a whole is set in Arcadia, either literally or metaphorically. If, as Bruno Snell maintains, it was indeed Virgil who discovered 'Arcadia', then, as Mahaffy argued a century ago, it was Iacopo Sannazaro who colonized that land and gave it its modern connotation, when he published his pastoral romance of that name in verse and prose at Naples in 1504.[10]

For in fact (with due apologies to all true believers in Arcadia, the 'bower' and the 'pleasaunce', and that dreary *locus amoenus* misbegotten out of Isidore by Ernst Robert Curtius)[11] Virgil's pastoral world suffers from two major evils, a public and a private.

The first of these provides the background for *Eclogues* I, IV and IX; the second is the real subject of *Eclogues* II, VI, VIII and X. The landscape of the *Eclogues* has not, like the countryside of *Georgics* I, been ravaged by war, nor, despite the terror that grips the world, is the tramp of marching legions heard along the pastoral highways. What has happened is the forcible transfer of land from the possession of its former owners and tenants into the hands of soldiers demobilized by their victorious commanders. Poetry can be used as a means of appeal to the authorities presiding over this ruthless re-allocation, but such poetical appeals must often fail and the shepherds recognize that poetry is powerless in a world ruled by the War God, Mars. Virgil himself sees the best hope for the future peace and pros-

9. See Isidore, *Etymologiae*, VIII.6.12, who reports Democritus, the pre-Socratic philosopher, as saying: 'Truth lies hidden, as though in a deep unfathomable well.'

10. Snell (1953), p. 281 and Mahaffy (1887), pp. 303–8; I owe the latter reference to Dr Ernst Schmidt.

11. For these terms consult the index to Rosenmeyer (1969) and see Curtius (1953), p. 192 for a misreading of Isidore XIV.8.33 and Horace *Ars Poetica* 17.

perity of the Roman people in the rule of one man, offspring of the dynastic marriage agreed at Brindisi.[12] Presumably he was not the only Roman citizen to hold this view, for Julius Caesar's autocracy had met with strong popular support. *Eclogue* IV is interesting evidence that as early as 40 BC people were thinking in these terms, and it makes it easier for us to understand how the young man whom Tityrus worships as a god in *Eclogue* I could be accepted in 27 BC as virtual sole ruler of the Roman empire.

So much for the public evil, civil war and its results. The private evil was even older and more refractory, although in our technological society it is regarded not only as a blessing but as an essential ingredient of the happy life – something, indeed, which every self-respecting young person will now claim to have experienced. But in antiquity the thing was madness. Offspring of Chaos, it darkened the wisdom of the Almighty Father Himself.[13] Such at least was the teaching of the earliest Greek poets, and most philosophers, including the Stoics and Epicureans, gave passionate love (Greek *eros*, Latin *amor*) a very bad name, regarding the condition as a form of disease, for which they were careful to prescribe a philosophical cure. The Epicurean view of *amor* finds its most powerful expression in the last two hundred lines of the fourth book of Lucretius's *On the Nature of Things*. Tradition, as we have seen, reports that Virgil was drawn to the Epicurean philosophy, and it is clear from numerous verbal similarities in the *Eclogues* that he had read Lucretius's great poem with the closest attention. If we can take passages such as *Eclogue* VIII 41–50 as representing his own view, then he evidently regarded passionate love as a dire misfortune, if not a moral evil (his description of it as *malus error*, even in context, is somewhat ambiguous). Now, Theocritus had a remedy for this wretched condition, as he tells his doctor friend at the beginning of *Idyll* XI: he prescribes 'the

12. See Du Quesnay (1976), p. 84.

13. At Homer, *Iliad* XIV.294 Zeus sees Hera, who is wearing the irresistible girdle (*kestos*) of Aphrodite, and 'when he saw, then Eros overlaid his wits'.

Muses', by which he means, as is clear from what follows, not the reading but the writing of poetry. Virgil, however, is less optimistic and has no remedy to offer – unless we read the opening lines of *Eclogue* II as implicitly saying that if you express your passion often enough in your own home-made poetry you will eventually, like Corydon, come to your senses or (perhaps better) to your right mind. The interesting thing is that Virgil's geographical Arcadia in *Eclogue* X (once again the exception) is free from the scourge, not of 'love', but of unrequited 'love'. Gallus, who is dying of that complaint, has somehow found his way there and announces to its inhabitants that, had he been an Arcadian field-worker suffering from love's madness (*furor*), the object of his passion would have consoled him as they lay together 'among willows, under a limber vine' – with a bunch of flowers or a song.

The three remaining *Eclogues* (III, V and VII) with their answering, or amoebean, songs can be classed together under the heading of competition.[14] Now, competition was un-Epicurean; the Master, like some modern educationists and other utopians, though for a different reason, regarded it as a bad thing. 'The man', he writes, 'who recognizes life's limits knows how easy it is to remove all pain caused by want and to make one's whole life complete, so he has no need of things that involve competition (*agonas*, 'contests').'[15] Are we to take this emphasis on competition as Virgil's independent answer to 'the problem' of our aggressive instincts? Is he perhaps saying to us, indirectly, 'Make verse, not war'? Quite honestly, it is simpler to think that he is following the precedent of Greek pastoral, for competition is as prominent in the *Idylls*. When young Menalcas loses in *Idyll* VIII he takes it very badly and 'smoulders with resentment' (not exactly an Arcadian reaction, perhaps). Simi-

14. Servius on *Eclogue* II.38: '*Amoebean* is when the singers use the same number of verses and the respondent either caps what has been said or contradicts it.'

15. Epicurus, *Principal Doctrines*, 21.

larly, in *Eclogue* V, young Mopsus is highly indignant when Amyntas is said to be his equal, and in his indignation unconsciously puts himself on a par with Phoebus, the god of poetry. And competition probably came into the *Idylls* from real life: it is not difficult to believe that ancient shepherds competed in song and undoubtedly ancient poets were a competitive lot.[16] In *Idyll* VII Simichidas (Theocritus) recognizes that as yet he is no match for the older poets Asclepiades and Philetas, and Lycidas expresses his detestation of those contemporaries who try to rival Homer. Similarly, Virgil in *Eclogue* IX, speaking through the mouth of Lycidas, admits that his work is not yet up to that of Varius and Cinna, and in *Eclogue* III not only puffs Pollio's latest composition but takes a swipe at Bavius and Maevius, contemporaries who, it appears, were unwise enough to lampoon him and his friend Horace and who have in consequence gone down to posterity as poetasters *par excellence*.

But the most striking example of this competitive spirit occurs in *Eclogue* IV. The poet prays for a life long enough to celebrate the achievements of the male child to be born to Mark Antony and Octavia, and claims that then he would not only be a match for the legendary singers Orpheus and Linus but would actually defeat the god Pan himself, even though Arcadia (Pan's own country) were judging the competition. The more one thinks about this passage the more surprising it seems. Clearly in Virgil's time 'great Pan is dead',[17] otherwise such talk would be extremely unwise, for the gods are notoriously jealous and Pan in particular a most dangerous and unpredictable character.

16. Compare Hesiod *Works and Days*, 26: 'And beggar envies beggar and bard bard'.

17. Plutarch reports that a voice was heard announcing this in the reign of Tiberius: see his *Defence of Oracles*, [17] 419. Alternatively, Virgil, as a good Epicurean, would hold that the Gods, whose divine forms were known to human beings 'by clear vision' and who lived in the *intermundia*, or 'spaces between the worlds', could never be angry or jealous; see the very interesting passage where Lucretius stresses the importance for human happiness of a correct conception of the Gods (*De Rerum Natura* VI.68–79), and Bailey's notes.

Virgil goes a great deal further here than Moschus in his *Lament for Bion*, the dead pastoral poet (51–2, 55–6):

> Who, O thrice desired, will ever play thy syrinx?
> Who set lip to thy reeds? Who so presumptuous? ...
> Do I take thy pipe to Pan? Even he perhaps will fear
> To press his lip there, lest he take second prize to thee.

The great in Virgil's time were colloquially known as 'gods' (for instance, Horace *Satires* II.6.52), and poets burnt the incense of panegyric for their noble nostrils. Virgil is not primarily blowing his own pan-pipe here, though clearly he *is* doing that; but his purpose, apart from expressing his longing for a world at peace, is indirect praise of Antony and Octavia and, through her, of her brother Octavian.

Fortunately these reflexions do not arise while one reads the poem, for then one is under the spell of the music and movement of its verse. Virgil's *Eclogues* are, above all, incantatory poetry, and from the reader's point of view incantation inhibits thought. The incantation mainly depends on three things: first, the *cantabile* element mentioned earlier; secondly, the repetition of words and phrases; and thirdly, antithesis. A good example of all three elements in combination will be found in the last eleven lines of *Eclogue* IV. Anyone who reads the Latin aloud cannot fail to hear its *cantabile* or to notice the various repetitions. One might, however, miss the antitheses between *mihi* and *tua* in 53–4, *puer* and *matrem* in 60, *puer* and *parenti* in 62, though the double antitheses in 57 and 63 are obvious enough. But it is now high time to close this introduction, whose beginning, middle and end have emphasized the poetry of the *Eclogues*, and to venture the hope that the reader will find them as enthralling as has the translator.

THE ECLOGUES

ECLOGUE I

The subject is announced in the first five lines; the remainder of the *Eclogue* fills in that outline with vivid details about the two contrasting characters, their past, present and future. Tityrus's rustic refusal to answer a straight question, his naive impressions of Rome, and revelations about his love-life, provide the humour; Meliboeus's eviction provides the pathos.

Antiquity was convinced that Tityrus was Virgil and the poem autobiography in disguise: according to that reading the poet's family farm had been confiscated after Philippi (see note on line 70) but restored to him by the young Octavian (see note on 41–2), who is then thanked by this poem. We are more sceptical. Winterbottom (1976), p. 56, takes it as containing not only eulogy of Octavian but also political protest against the land-confiscations; Virgil is Tityrus in the sense that he is unscathed by the power-politics of the day and can sit in his study composing bucolic poetry. See also Wilkinson (1969), pp. 28–35 and Du Quesnay (1981).

Robert Frost's 'Build Soil! – A Political Pastoral', and Louis Macneice's 'An Eclogue for Christmas' are modern descendants; truest to life is the mid-nineteenth-century *Eclogue* in the Dorset dialect by William Barnes, '*Rusticus Emigrans* – Emigration', beginning:

> Well Richat, zoo 'tis true what I do hear
> That you be guoin' to Dieman's Land to-year.

ECLOGA I

MELIBOEVS TITYRVS

M. Tityre, tu patulae recubans sub tegmine fagi
siluestrem tenui Musam meditaris auena;
nos patriae finis et dulcia linquimus arua.
nos patriam fugimus; tu, Tityre, lentus in umbra
formosam resonare doces Amaryllida siluas.
T. O Meliboee, deus nobis haec otia fecit.
namque erit ille mihi semper deus, illius aram
saepe tener nostris ab ouilibus imbuet agnus.
ille meas errare boues, ut cernis, et ipsum
ludere quae uellem calamo permisit agresti.
M. Non equidem inuideo, miror magis: undique totis
usque adeo turbatur agris. en ipse capellas
protinus aeger ago; hanc etiam uix, Tityre, duco.
hic inter densas corylos modo namque gemellos,
spem gregis, a! silice in nuda conixa reliquit.
saepe malum hoc nobis, si mens non laeua fuisset,
de caelo tactas memini praedicere quercus.
sed tamen iste deus qui sit, da, Tityre, nobis.
T. Vrbem quam dicunt Romam, Meliboee, putaui
stultus ego huic nostrae similem, quo saepe solemus
pastores ouium teneros depellere fetus.
sic canibus catulos similis, sic matribus haedos
noram, sic paruis componere magna solebam.
uerum haec tantum alias inter caput extulit urbes
quantum lenta solent inter uiburna cupressi.
M. Et quae tanta fuit Romam tibi causa uidendi?
T. Libertas, quae sera tamen respexit inertem,
candidior postquam tondenti barba cadebat,
respexit tamen et longo post tempore uenit,
postquam nos Amaryllis habet, Galatea reliquit.
namque (fatebor enim) dum me Galatea tenebat,
nec spes libertatis erat nec cura peculi.
quamuis multa meis exiret uictima saeptis,

ECLOGUE I

MELIBOEUS TITYRUS

M. Tityrus, lying back beneath wide beechen cover,
You meditate the woodland Muse on slender oat;
We leave the boundaries and sweet ploughlands of home.
We flee our homeland; you, Tityrus, cool in shade,
Are teaching woods to echo *Lovely Amaryllis.*
T. Oh, Meliboéus, a god has made this leisure ours.
Yes, he will always be a god for me; his altar
A tender ram-lamb from our folds will often stain.
He has allowed, as you can see, my cows to range
And me to play what tune I please on the wild reed.
M. I am not envious, more amazed: the countryside's
All in such turmoil. Sick myself, look, Tityrus,
I drive goats forward; this one I can hardly lead.
For here in the hazel thicket just now dropping twins,
Ah, the flock's hope, on naked flint, she abandoned them.
I keep remembering how the oak-trees touched of heaven,
If we had been right-minded, foretold this evil time.
But give us that god of yours: who is he, Tityrus?
T. The city men call Rome I reckoned, Meliboéus,
Fool that I was, like this of ours, to which we shepherds
Are often wont to drive the weanlings of the ewes.
So puppies are like dogs, I knew, so kids are like
Their mother goats, so I'd compare big things to small.
But she has raised her head among the other cities
High as a cypress-tree above the guelder-rose.
M. And what was your great reason, then, for seeing Rome?
T. Liberty, which, though late, looked kindly on the indolent,
After my beard fell whiter to the barber's trim,
Looked kindly, though, and after a long while arrived,
After Amaryllis had us and Galatéa left.
For (yes, I will confess) while Galatea held me,
There was no hope of liberty nor thought of thrift.
Though many a sacrificial victim left my pens,

pinguis et ingratae premeretur caseus urbi,
non umquam grauis aere domum mihi dextra redibat.
M. Mirabar quid maesta deos, Amarylli, uocares,
cui pendere sua patereris in arbore poma;
Tityrus hinc aberat. ipsae te, Tityre, pinus,
ipsi te fontes, ipsa haec arbusta uocabant.
T. Quid facerem? neque seruitio me exire licebat
nec tam praesentis alibi cognoscere diuos.
hic illum uidi iuuenem, Meliboee, quotannis
bis senos cui nostra dies altaria fumant.
hic mihi responsum primus dedit ille petenti:
'pascite ut ante boues, pueri; summittite tauros.'
M. Fortunate senex, ergo tua rura manebunt
et tibi magna satis, quamuis lapis omnia nudus
limosoque palus obducat pascua iunco:
non insueta grauis temptabunt pabula fetas,
nec mala uicini pecoris contagia laedent.
fortunate senex, hic inter flumina nota
et fontis sacros frigus captabis opacum;
hinc tibi, quae semper, uicino ab limite saepes
Hyblaeis apibus florem depasta salicti
saepe leui somnum suadebit inire susurro;
hinc alta sub rupe canet frondator ad auras,
nec tamen interea raucae, tua cura, palumbes
nec gemere aeria cessabit turtur ab ulmo.
T. Ante leues ergo pascentur in aethere cerui
et freta destituent nudos in litore piscis,
ante pererratis amborum finibus exsul
aut Ararim Parthus bibet aut Germania Tigrim,
quam nostro illius labatur pectore uultus.
M. At nos hinc alii sitientis ibimus Afros,
pars Scythiam et rapidum cretae ueniemus Oaxen
et penitus toto diuisos orbe Britannos.
en umquam patrios longo post tempore finis
pauperis et tuguri congestum caespite culmen,

And much cream cheese was pressed for the ungrateful city,
My right hand never came back home heavy with bronze.
M. I wondered, Amaryllis, why you wept and called
To the gods – for whom you left fruit hanging on the tree;
Tityrus was away. The very pines, Tityrus,
The very springs, these very orchards called to you.
T. What could I do? For nowhere else could I escape
From slavery or meet divinities so present.
It was here I saw him, Meliboeus, the young man
For whom twice six days every year our altar smokes.
It was here to my petition he first gave reply:
'Graze cattle as before, my children, and yoke bulls.'
M. Lucky old man, the land then will remain your own,
And large enough for you, although bare rock and bog
With muddy rushes covers all the pasturage:
No unaccustomed feed will try your breeding ewes,
And no infection harm them from a neighbour's flock.
Lucky old man, among familiar rivers here
And sacred springs you'll angle for the cooling shade;
The hedge this side, along your neighbour's boundary,
Its willow flowers as ever feeding Hybla bees,
Will often whisper you persuasively to sleep;
The pruner under that high bluff will sing to the breeze,
Nor yet meanwhile will cooing pigeons, your own brood,
Nor turtledove be slow to moan from the airy elm.
T. Then sooner will light-footed stags feed in the sky
And ocean tides leave fishes naked on the shore,
Sooner in exile, wandering through each other's land,
Will Parthian drink the Arar, or Germany the Tigris,
Than from our memory will his face ever fade.
M. But *we* must leave here, some for thirsty Africa,
Others for Scythia and Oäxes' chalky flood
And the Britanni quite cut off from the whole world.
Look, shall I ever, seeing after a long while
My fathers' bounds and my poor cabin's turf-heaped roof,

post aliquot, mea regna, uidens mirabor aristas?
impius haec tam culta noualia miles habebit,
barbarus has segetes. en quo discordia ciuis
produxit miseros: his nos conseuimus agros!
insere nunc, Meliboee, piros, pone ordine uitis.
ite meae, felix quondam pecus, ite capellae.
non ego uos posthac uiridi proiectus in antro
dumosa pendere procul de rupe uidebo;
carmina nulla canam; non me pascente, capellae,
florentem cytisum et salices carpetis amaras.

T. Hic tamen hanc mecum poteras requiescere noctem
fronde super uiridi: sunt nobis mitia poma,
castaneae molles et pressi copia lactis,
et iam summa procul uillarum culmina fumant
maioresque cadunt altis de montibus umbrae.

Hereafter marvel at my kingdom – a few corn-ears?
Some godless veteran will own this fallow tilth,
These cornfields a barbarian. Look where strife has led
Rome's wretched citizens: we have sown fields for these!
Graft pear trees, Meliboeus, now, set vines in rows.
Go, little she-goats, go, once happy flock of mine.
Not I hereafter, stretched full length in some green cave,
Shall watch you far off hanging on a thorny crag;
I'll sing no songs; not in my keeping, little goats,
You'll crop the flowering lucerne and bitter willow.

T. However, for tonight you could rest here with me
Upon green leafage: I can offer you ripe fruit
And mealy chestnuts and abundance of milk cheese.
Far off the roof-tops of the farms already smoke
And down from the high mountains taller shadows fall.

ECLOGUE II

Corydon *solo* talks to Alexis as though he were present, appealing, admonishing and (as he thinks) enticing; at line 56 he looks inward, reasoning with himself, outward again at 60, then again inward at 69, where he recognizes his irrationality and remembers the everyday chores that need doing. This incongruous behaviour together with his incongruous character (at once naive and sophisticated: see, for instance, 25–6 and 24) is humorous in effect; at the same time the poem shows real insight into the mind of the rejected lover, into the fantasy world he creates for himself. Virgil takes the then familiar idea of love as madness (69 *dementia*) and shows how it works, not as an Epicurean or a satirist would, but as a poet who understands and sympathizes. See also introduction, p. 23, and Du Quesnay (1979).

Ancient readers interpreted the poem autobiographically: for them Corydon was Virgil and Alexis a beautiful slave-boy named Alexander, allegedly given to the poet by his patron Pollio.

Eliot's 'The Love Song of J. Alfred Prufrock' is a modern analogue, and Spenser's 'First Aeglogue: Januarye' an Elizabethan descendant.

Formosum pastor Corydon ardebat Alexin,
delicias domini, nec quid speraret habebat.
tantum inter densas, umbrosa cacumina, fagos
adsidue ueniebat. ibi haec incondita solus
montibus et siluis studio iactabat inani;
'O crudelis Alexi, nihil mea carmina curas?
nil nostri miserere? mori me denique coges.
nunc etiam pecudes umbras et frigora captant,
nunc uiridis etiam occultant spineta lacertos,
Thestylis et rapido fessis messoribus aestu
alia serpyllumque herbas contundit olentis.
at mecum raucis, tua dum uestigia lustro,
sole sub ardenti resonant arbusta cicadis.
nonne fuit satius tristis Amaryllidis iras
atque superba pati fastidia? nonne Menalcan,
quamuis ille niger, quamuis tu candidus esses?
o formose puer, nimium ne crede colori:
alba ligustra cadunt, uaccinia nigra leguntur.
despectus tibi sum, nec qui sim quaeris, Alexi,
quam diues pecoris, niuei quam lactis abundans.
mille meae Siculis errant in montibus agnae;
lac mihi non aestate nouum, non frigore defit.
canto quae solitus, si quando armenta uocabat,
Amphion Dircaeus in Actaeo Aracyntho.
nec sum adeo informis: nuper me in litore uidi,
cum placidum uentis staret mare. non ego Daphnin
iudice te metuam, si numquam fallit imago.
o tantum libeat mecum tibi sordida rura
atque humilis habitare casas et figere ceruos,
haedorumque gregem uiridi compellere hibisco!
mecum una in siluis imitabere Pana canendo
(Pan primum calamos cera coniungere pluris
instituit, Pan curat ouis ouiumque magistros),
nec te paeniteat calamo triuisse labellum:
haec eadem ut sciret, quid non faciebat Amyntas?

For beautiful Alexis, the master's favourite,
Shepherd Córydon burned, and knew he had no hope.
Only, he used to walk each day among the dense
Shady-topped beeches. There, alone, in empty longing,
He hurled this artless monologue at hills and woods:
'O cruel Alexis, have you no time for my tunes?
No pity for us? You'll be the death of me at last.
Now, even the cattle cast about for cool and shade,
Now even green lizards hide among the hawthorn brakes,
And Thestylis, for reapers faint from the fierce heat,
Is crushing pungent pot-herbs, garlic and wild thyme.
But I, while vineyards ring with the cicadas' scream,
Retrace your steps, alone, beneath the burning sun.
Had I not better bide the wrath of Amaryllis,
Her high-and-mighty moods? Better endure Menalcas,
However black he were and you however blond?
O lovely boy, don't trust complexion overmuch:
White privet flowers fall, black bilberries are picked.
You scorn me, Alexis, never asking who I am,
How rich in flocks, how affluent in snowy milk.
My thousand ewe-lambs range the hills of Sicily;
Come frost, come summer, never do I lack fresh milk.
I play the tunes Amphíon used, when he called cattle,
Dircéan Amphion on Actéan Aracýnthus.
I'm not that ugly: on the beach I saw myself
Lately, when sea stood wind-becalmed. With you as judge
I'd not be scared of Daphnis, if mirrors tell the truth.
O if you'd only fancy life with me in country
Squalor, in a humble hut, and shooting fallow deer,
And shepherding a flock of kids with green hibiscus!
Piping beside me in the woods you'll mimic Pan
(Pan pioneered the fixing fast of several reeds
With bees-wax; sheep are in Pan's care, head-shepherds too);
You'd not be sorry when the reed callused your lip:
What pains Amyntas took to master this same art!

est mihi disparibus septem compacta cicutis
fistula, Damoetas dono mihi quam dedit olim,
et dixit moriens: 'te nunc habet ista secundum';
dixit Damoetas, inuidit stultus Amyntas.
praeterea duo nec tuta mihi ualle reperti
capreoli, sparsis etiam nunc pellibus albo,
bina die siccant ouis ubera; quos tibi seruo.
iam pridem a me illos abducere Thestylis orat;
et faciet, quoniam sordent tibi munera nostra.
huc ades, o formose puer: tibi lilia plenis
ecce ferunt Nymphae calathis; tibi candida Nais,
pallentis uiolas et summa papauera carpens,
narcissum et florem iungit bene olentis anethi;
tum casia atque aliis intexens suauibus herbis
mollia luteola pingit uaccinia calta.
ipse ego cana legam tenera lanugine mala
castaneasque nuces, mea quas Amaryllis amabat;
addam cerea pruna (honos erit huic quoque pomo),
et uos, o lauri, carpam et te, proxima myrte,
sic positae quoniam suauis miscetis odores.
rusticus es, Corydon; nec munera curat Alexis,
nec, si muneribus certes, concedat Iollas.
heu heu, quid uolui misero mihi? floribus Austrum
perditus et liquidis immisi fontibus apros.
quem fugis, a! demens? habitarunt di quoque siluas
Dardaniusque Paris. Pallas quas condidit arces
ipsa colat; nobis placeant ante omnia siluae.
torua leaena lupum sequitur, lupus ipse capellam,
florentem cytisum sequitur lasciua capella,
te Corydon, o Alexi: trahit sua quemque uoluptas.
aspice, aratra iugo referunt suspensa iuuenci,
et sol crescentis decedens duplicat umbras;
me tamen urit amor: quis enim modus adsit amori?
a Corydon, Corydon, quae te dementia cepit!
semiputata tibi frondosa uitis in ulmo est:

I have a pipe composed of seven unequal stems
Of hemlock, which Damoetas gave me when he died,
A while ago, and said, "Now she owns you, the second,'
Damoetas said; Amyntas envied me, the fool.
Two chamois kids, besides, I found in a sheer coomb.
Their hides are dappled even now with white; they drain
One ewe's dugs each a day; I'm keeping them for you,
Though Thestylis has long desired to take them from me;
She'll do it too, since you regard our gifts as crude.
Come here, O lovely boy: for you the Nymphs bring lilies,
Look, in baskets full; for you the Naiad fair,
Plucking pale violets and poppy heads, combines
Narcissus with them, and the flower of fragrant dill;
Then, weaving marjoram in, and other pleasant herbs,
Colours soft bilberries with yellow marigold.
Myself, I'll pick the grey-white apples with tender down,
And chestnuts, which my Amaryllis used to love;
I'll add the waxy plum (this fruit too shall be honoured),
And I'll pluck you, O laurels, and you, neighbour myrtle,
For so arranged you mingle pleasant fragrances.
Corydon, you're a yokel; Alexis scorns your gifts,
Nor could you beat Iollas in a giving-match.
Alas, what have I done, poor lunatic, unleashing
Auster on flower-beds and wild boar on clear springs!
Ah, you are mad to leave me. Gods have dwelt in woods,
Dardanian Paris too. Pallas can keep her cities,
But let the woods beyond all else please you and me.
Grim lions pursue the wolf, wolves in their turn the goat,
Mischievous goats pursue the flowering lucerne,
And Corydon you, Alexis – each at pleasure's pull.
Look, oxen now bring home their yoke-suspended ploughs,
And the sun, going down, doubles growing shadows;
But I burn in love's fire: can one set bounds to love?
Ah, Corydon, Corydon, what madness mastered you!
You've left a vine half-pruned upon a leafy elm:

quin tu aliquid saltem potius, quorum indiget usus,
uiminibus mollique paras detexere iunco?
inuenies alium, si te hic fastidit, Alexin.'

Why not at least prepare to weave of osiers
And supple rushes something practical you need?
If this Alexis sneers at you, you'll find another.'

ECLOGUE III

Two shepherds meet and taunt each other with accusations of theft, sexual perversion, malicious damage to property, jealousy and musical incompetence. The elder challenges the younger to a singing-match; the stake is agreed and a judge found. The contest, in answering couplets, consists of twelve rounds, or twenty-four couplets. The judge pronounces it a draw.

This was probably Virgil's earliest *Eclogue*, for it is the closest of all to Theocritus, being based on *Idyll* V (fourteen rounds of answering couplets) with passages adapted from other *Idylls*. Virgil makes the shepherds devote two rounds to Pollio, thereby including a humorous compliment, indeed a dedication, to his patron. For the best discussion see Currie (1976).

There is a good nineteenth-century slanging-match in William Barnes, 'Eclogue: The Best Man in the Vield', beginning:

> That's slowish work, Bob. What'st a-been about?
> Thy pooken don't goo on not over sprack.

MENALCAS DAMOETAS PALAEMON

M. Dic mihi, Damoeta, cuium pecus? an Meliboei?
D. Non, uerum Aegonis; nuper mihi tradidit Aegon.
M. Infelix o semper, oues, pecus! ipse Neaeram
dum fouet ac ne me sibi praeferat illa ueretur,
hic alienus ouis custos bis mulget in hora,
et sucus pecori et lac subducitur agnis.
D. Parcius ista uiris tamen obicienda memento.
nouimus et qui te transuersa tuentibus hircis
et quo (sed faciles Nymphae risere) sacello.
M. Tum, credo, cum me arbustum uidere Miconis
atque mala uitis incidere falce nouellas.
D. Aut hic ad ueteres fagos cum Daphnidis arcum
fregisti et calamos: quae tu, peruerse Menalca,
et cum uidisti puero donata, dolebas,
et si non aliqua nocuisses, mortuus esses.
M. Quid domini faciant, audent cum talia fures?
non ego te uidi Damonis, pessime, caprum
excipere insidiis multum latrante Lycisca?
et cum clamarem 'quo nunc se proripit ille?
Tityre, coge pecus', tu post carecta latebas.
D. An mihi cantando uictus non redderet ille,
quem mea carminibus meruisset fistula caprum?
si nescis, meus ille caper fuit; et mihi Damon
ipse fatebatur, sed reddere posse negabat.
M. Cantando tu illum? aut umquam tibi fistula cera
iuncta fuit? non tu in triuiis, indocte, solebas
stridenti miserum stipula disperdere carmen?
D. Vis ergo inter nos quid possit uterque uicissim
experiamur? ego hanc uitulam (ne forte recuses,
bis uenit ad mulctram, binos alit ubere fetus)
depono; tu dic mecum quo pignore certes.
M. De grege non ausim quicquam deponere tecum:
est mihi namque domi pater, est iniusta nouerca,

ECLOGUE III

MENALCAS DAMOETAS PALAEMON

M. Tell me, Damoetas – whose flock? Meliboeus his?
D. No, Aegon's; Aegon left me in charge not long ago.
M. Poor sheep! That flock's always unlucky. While himself
Fondles Neaera, dreading that she favours me,
This hired keeper drains the ewes dry twice an hour,
Robbing the flock of all their sap, the lambs of milk.
D. Watch what you say, before accusing *men* of that.
We know what you did, while the he-goats looked and leered,
And in a shrine too, though the easy Wood-Nymphs laughed.
M. The day, no doubt, they saw *me* hacking Mico's trees
And tender vine-shoots with a spiteful pruning-hook.
D. Or right here, by the old beeches, breaking Daphnis' bow
And his cane-arrows; for it riled your twisted mind,
Menalcas, when you saw the boy presented with them,
And if you hadn't hurt him somehow, you'd have died.
M. What can employers do, when thieves are so bare-faced?
You scoundrel, didn't I see you lie in wait and catch
That goat of Damon's, while Lycisca barked and barked?
And when I shouted 'Where's that fellow off to now?
Tityrus, watch your flock!' you lay low in the sedge.
D. I'd beaten him at playing. Wasn't he to pay
The billy-goat my pan-pipe earned me with its tunes?
If you don't know, that goat was mine. Damon himself
Admitted it to me, but said he couldn't pay.
M. Beat him at playing – you? Or have you ever owned
A wax-joined pan-pipe? Dunce, at the crossroads wasn't it you
Who murdered miserable tunes on squeaking straw?
D. Then would you like the two of us in turn to try
What each can do? This heifer here (now don't say no –
She comes to the milk-pail twice a day, suckles twin calves)
Is my stake. You say what you're betting on our match.
M. I dare not wager any of the flock with you:
There's father, there's my unjust stepmother at home,

bisque die numerant ambo pecus, alter et haedos.
uerum, id quod multo tute ipse fatebere maius
(insanire libet quoniam tibi), pocula ponam
fagina, caelatum diuini opus Alcimedontis,
lenta quibus torno facili superaddita uitis
diffusos hedera uestit pallente corymbos.
in medio duo signa, Conon et – quis fuit alter,
descripsit radio totum qui gentibus orbem,
tempora quae messor, quae curuus arator haberet?
necdum illis labra admoui, sed condita seruo.

D. Et nobis idem Alcimedon duo pocula fecit
et molli circum est ansas amplexus acantho,
Orpheaque in medio posuit siluasque sequentis;
necdum illis labra admoui, sed condita seruo.
si ad uitulam spectas, nihil est quod pocula laudes.

M. Numquam hodie effugies; ueniam quocumque uocaris.
audiat haec tantum – uel qui uenit ecce Palaemon.
efficiam posthac ne quemquam uoce lacessas.

D. Quin age, si quid habes; in me mora non erit ulla,
nec quemquam fugio: tantum, uicine Palaemon,
sensibus haec imis (res est non parua) reponas.

P. Dicite, quandoquidem in molli consedimus herba.
et nunc omnis ager, nunc omnis parturit arbos,
nunc frondent siluae, nunc formosissimus annus.
incipe, Damoeta; tu deinde sequere, Menalca.
alternis dicetis; amant alterna Camenae.

D. Ab Ioue principium Musae: Iouis omnia plena;
ille colit terras, illi mea carmina curae.

M. Et me Phoebus amat; Phoebo sua semper apud me
munera sunt, lauri et suaue rubens hyacinthus.

D. Malo me Galatea petit, lasciua puella,
et fugit ad salices et se cupit ante uideri.

M. At mihi sese offert ultro, meus ignis, Amyntas,
notior ut iam sit canibus non Delia nostris.

D. Parta meae Veneri sunt munera: namque notaui

And twice a day both count the goats, and one the kids.
But here's what even you will admit is worth far more:
As you're so keen to play the fool, I'll lay these beechwood
Cups, embossed work of divine Alcimedon,
On which a lithe vine, added by his easy lathe,
Is clothing berry-clusters scattered on pale ivy.
Two central figures: Conon and – who was the other,
Who marked out with his rod the whole round for mankind,
What times the reaper keeps, and what the stooping ploughman?
I've not yet put them to my lips, but keep them by.

D. The same Alcimedon also made two cups for us,
And twining soft acanthus leaves around the handles
Placed Orpheus in the centre and forests following;
I've not yet put them to my lips, but keep them by.
Look at the heifer, though. No cause to praise the cups.

M. You'll never escape today. I'll answer every call.
Only, we need a judge – look, here's Palaemon coming.
I'll make quite sure you challenge no one after this.

D. Then come on, if you've anything. I'll not hold back,
And no one scares me off: only, neighbour Palaemon,
Lay these songs (it's no light matter) deeply to heart.

P. Sing then, because we sit together on soft grass,
And every field now, every tree is burgeoning;
Now woods are leafing, now the year is loveliest.
Begin, Damoetas. You, Menalcas, follow on
Capping. You'll sing in turn. Camenae love their turns.

D. With Jove the Muse begins: all things are full of Jove;
He cultivates the earth, my couplets are his care.

M. And Phoebus loves me; I keep fitting gifts at home
For Phoebus, bay and sweetly blushing hyacinth.

D. Galatea, the cheeky girl, pelts me with apples,
Runs to the sally beds, and longs to be seen first.

M. My flame Amyntas gives himself to me unasked;
Not even Delia's more familiar to our dogs.

D. Presents are laid up for my Venus: I myself

ipse locum, aëriae quo congessere palumbes.
M. Quod potui, puero siluestri ex arbore lecta
aurea mala decem misi; cras altera mittam.
D. O quotiens et quae nobis Galatea locuta est!
partem aliquam, uenti, diuum referatis ad auris!
M. Quid prodest quod me ipse animo non spernis, Amynta,
si, dum tu sectaris apros, ego retia seruo?
D. Phyllida mitte mihi: meus est natalis, Iolla;
cum faciam uitula pro frugibus, ipse uenito.
M. Phyllida amo ante alias; nam me discedere fleuit
et 'longum, formose, uale, uale' inquit, Iolla.
D. Triste lupus stabulis, maturis frugibus imbres,
arboribus uenti, nobis Amaryllidis irae.
M. Dulce satis umor, depulsis arbutus haedis,
lenta salix feto pecori, mihi solus Amyntas.
D. Pollio amat nostram, quamuis est rustica, Musam:
Pierides, uitulam lectori pascite uestro.
M. Pollio et ipse facit noua carmina: pascite taurum,
iam cornu petat et pedibus qui spargat harenam.
D. Qui te, Pollio, amat, ueniat quo te quoque gaudet;
mella fluant illi, ferat et rubus asper amomum.
M. Qui Bauium non odit, amet tua carmina, Maeui,
atque idem iungat uulpes et mulgeat hircos.
D. Qui legitis flores et humi nascentia fraga,
frigidus, o pueri (fugite hinc!), latet anguis in herba.
M. Parcite, oues, nimium procedere: non bene ripae
creditur; ipse aries etiam nunc uellera siccat.
D. Tityre, pascentis a flumine reice capellas:
ipse, ubi tempus erit, omnis in fonte lauabo.
M. Cogite ouis, pueri: si lac praeceperit aestus,
ut nuper, frustra pressabimus ubera palmis.
D. Heu heu, quam pingui macer est mihi taurus in eruo!
idem amor exitium pecori pecorisque magistro.
M. His certe (neque amor causa est) uix ossibus haerent;
nescio quis teneros oculus mihi fascinat agnos.

Observed the place where the airy wood-pigeons have built.
M. The best I could I've sent the boy – ten golden apples
Picked from a woodland tree; I'll send ten more tomorrow.
D. Oh, Galatea has told us so much, and so often!
You breezes, waft a word or two to the gods' ears.
M. What good is it that you don't scorn me in your heart,
Amyntas, if, while you hunt boar, I mind the nets?
D. Iollas, it's my birthday; send me Phyllis now:
Then, when I kill the harvest heifer, come yourself.
M. Iollas, I love Phyllis most of all; for when
I left, she wept and said, 'So long, handsome, so long!'
D. Wolves are a sad thing for the folds, rain for ripe crops,
Gales for the trees, and Amaryllis' wrath for us.
M. Sweet to the sown is moisture, arbutus to weaned kids,
To brood-ewes pliant willow, Amyntas alone to me.
D. Pollio loves our Muse, bucolic though she be.
Fatten a heifer for your reader, Pierians.
M. Pollio makes new songs himself. Fatten a bull,
One old enough to toss his horns and paw the sand.
D. Let him who loves you, Pollio, share your paradise;
Let honey flow for him, and brambles bear spikenard.
M. Let him who hates not Bavius love Maevius' songs,
And likewise let him milk he-goats and yoke the fox.
D. You children picking flowers and earth-born strawberries,
Oh, run away; a cold snake's lurking in the grass.
M. Don't move ahead too far, my flock: it's dangerous
To trust the river bank; the ram's fleece is still wet.
D. Drive from the river, Tityrus, the grazing goats:
All in good time I'll dip them in the spring myself.
M. Round up the ewes, lads: if the heat should take their milk,
As happened lately, we'll be squeezing teats in vain.
D. Alas, alas, how lean my bull on that fat vetch!
Alike to herd and herdsman love is ruinous.
M. True, them are skin and bone, but love is not the cause;
Some evil eye has overlooked my tender lambs.

D. Dic quibus in terris (et eris mihi magnus Apollo)
tris pateat caeli spatium non amplius ulnas.
M. Dic quibus in terris inscripti nomina regum
nascantur flores, et Phyllida solus habeto.
P. Non nostrum inter uos tantas componere lites:
et uitula tu dignus et hic, et quisquis amores
aut metuet dulcis aut experietur amaros.
claudite iam riuos, pueri; sat prata biberunt.

D. Say in what lands (and you shall be my great Apollo)
The spacious sky extends no wider than three ells.
M. Say in what lands the flowers inscribed with names of kings
Are born, and you shall have our Phyllis to yourself.
P. Not ours to arbitrate these great disputes between you.
Both you and he have earned the heifer – so have all
Who fear the sweet or feel the bitterness of love.
Now close the sluices, lads; the fields have drunk their fill.

ECLOGUE IV

The Fourth is the famous Messianic *Eclogue*, which the Christian fathers Lactantius and Augustine and the medieval Church took as prefiguring the birth of Christ, and which the Emperor Constantine himself translated into Greek hexameters. Reference to the Virgin (6), the Serpent (24), the primal deceit (31), and similarities to Isaiah ix, 6 and xi, 6 and to ideas about the Millennium made a Christian interpretation inevitable.

The poem was probably written to celebrate the dynastic marriage of Antony and Octavia (see introduction, p. 20). For the best discussions see Williams (1974) and Du Quesnay (1976).

Shelley's final chorus from 'Hellas' (1822) can be compared:

> The world's great age begins anew,
> The golden years return ...

Sicelides Musae, paulo maiora canamus!
non omnis arbusta iuuant humilesque myricae;
si canimus siluas, siluae sint consule dignae.
  Vltima Cumaei uenit iam carminis aetas;
magnus ab integro saeclorum nascitur ordo.
iam redit et uirgo, redeunt Saturnia regna,
iam noua progenies caelo demittitur alto.
tu modo nascenti puero, quo ferrea primum
desinet ac toto surget gens aurea mundo,
casta faue Lucina: tuus iam regnat Apollo.
teque adeo decus hoc aeui, te consule, inibit,
Pollio, et incipient magni procedere menses;
te duce, si qua manent sceleris uestigia nostri,
inrita perpetua soluent formidine terras.
ille deum uitam accipiet diuisque uidebit
permixtos heroas et ipse uidebitur illis,
pacatumque reget patriis uirtutibus orbem.
  At tibi prima, puer, nullo munuscula cultu
errantis hederas passim cum baccare tellus
mixtaque ridenti colocasia fundet acantho.
ipsae lacte domum referent distenta capellae
ubera, nec magnos metuent armenta leones;
ipsa tibi blandos fundent cunabula flores.
occidet et serpens, et fallax herba ueneni
occidet; Assyrium uulgo nascetur amomum.
at simul heroum laudes et facta parentis
iam legere et quae sit poteris cognoscere uirtus,
molli paulatim flavescet campus arista
incultisque rubens pendebit sentibus uua
et durae quercus sudabunt roscida mella.
pauca tamen suberunt priscae uestigia fraudis,
quae temptare Thetim ratibus, quae cingere muris
oppida, quae iubeant telluri infindere sulcos.
alter erit tum Tiphys et altera quae uehat Argo
delectos heroas; erunt etiam altera bella

Sicilian Muses, grant me a slightly grander song.
Not all delight in trees and lowly tamarisks;
Let woods, if woods we sing, be worthy of a consul.
   Now the last age of Cumae's prophecy has come;
The great succession of centuries is born afresh.
Now too returns the Virgin; Saturn's rule returns;
A new begetting now descends from heaven's height.
O chaste Lucina, look with blessing on the boy
Whose birth will end the iron race at last and raise
A golden through the world: now your Apollo rules.
And, Pollio, this glory enters time with you;
Your consulship begins the march of the great months;
With you to guide, if traces of our sin remain,
They, nullified, will free the lands from lasting fear.
He will receive the life divine, and see the gods
Mingling with heroes, and himself be seen of them,
And rule a world made peaceful by his father's virtues.
   But first, as little gifts for you, child, Earth untilled
Will pour the straying ivy rife, and baccaris,
And colocasia mixing with acanthus' smile.
She-goats unshepherded will bring home udders plumped
With milk, and cattle will not fear the lion's might.
Your very cradle will pour forth caressing flowers.
The snake will perish, and the treacherous poison-herb
Perish; Assyrian spikenard commonly will grow.
And then, so soon as you can read of heroes' praise
And of your father's deeds, and know what manhood means,
Soft spikes of grain will gradually gild the fields,
And reddening grapes will hang in clusters on wild brier,
And dewy honey sweat from tough Italian oaks.
Traces, though few, will linger yet of the old deceit,
Commanding men to tempt Thetis with ships, to encircle
Towns with walls, to inflict deep furrows on the Earth.
There'll be a second Tiphys then, a second Argo
To carry chosen heroes; there'll even be second wars,

atque iterum ad Troiam magnus mittetur Achilles.
hinc, ubi iam firmata uirum te fecerit aetas,
cedet et ipse mari uector, nec nautica pinus
mutabit merces; omnis feret omnia tellus.
non rastros patietur humus, non uinea falcem;
robustus quoque iam tauris iuga soluet arator.
nec uarios discet mentiri lana colores,
ipse sed in pratis aries iam suaue rubenti
murice, iam croceo mutabit uellera luto;
sponte sua sandyx pascentis uestiet agnos.
'Talia saecla' suis dixerunt 'currite' fusis
concordes stabili fatorum numine Parcae.
adgredere o magnos (aderit iam tempus) honores,
cara deum suboles, magnum Iovis incrementum!
aspice conuexo nutantem pondere mundum,
terrasque tractusque maris caelumque profundum;
aspice, uenturo laetentur ut omnia saeclo!
o mihi tum longae maneat pars ultima uitae,
spiritus et quantum sat erit tua dicere facta!
non me carminibus uincet nec Thracius Orpheus
nec Linus, huic mater quamuis atque huic pater adsit,
Orphei Calliopea, Lino formosus Apollo.
Pan etiam, Arcadia mecum si iudice certet,
Pan etiam Arcadia dicat se iudice uictum.
Incipe, parue puer, risu cognoscere matrem
(matri longa decem tulerunt fastidia menses)
incipe, parue puer: qui non risere parenti,
nec deus hunc mensa, dea nec dignata cubili est.

And once more great Achilles will be sent to Troy.
Later, when strength of years has made a man of you,
The carrier too will quit the sea, no naval pines
Barter their goods, but every land bear everything.
The soil will suffer hoes no more, nor vines the hook.
The sturdy ploughman too will now unyoke his team,
And wool unlearn the lies of variable dye,
But in the fields the ram himself will change his fleece,
Now to sweet-blushing murex, now to saffron yellow,
And natural vermilion clothe the grazing lambs.
  'Speed on those centuries', said the Parcae to their spindles,
Concordant with the steadfast nod of Destiny.
O enter (for the time approaches) your great glory,
Dear scion of gods, great aftergrowth of Jupiter!
Look at the cosmos trembling in its massive round,
Lands and the expanse of ocean and the sky profound;
Look how they all are full of joy at the age to come!
O then for me may long life's latest part remain
And spirit great enough to celebrate your deeds!
Linus will not defeat me in song, nor Thracian Orpheûs,
Though one should have his father's aid and one his mother's,
Orpheus Callíopë and Linus fair Apollo.
If Pan too challenged me, with Arcady as judge,
Pan too, with Arcady as judge, would own defeat.
  Begin, small boy, to know your mother with a smile
(Ten lunar months have brought your mother long discomfort)
Begin, small boy: him who for parent have not smiled
No god invites to table nor goddess to bed.

ECLOGUE V

An elder shepherd, meeting a younger, pays him a compliment but only succeeds in giving offence. The younger sings a lament for the death of Daphnis which he has recently composed. After complimenting him again (perhaps tactlessly – 45, 'your song ... is like sleep') the elder replies with a song about Daphnis's apotheosis, which exactly balances the first, despite the fact that we are told it was composed earlier (13, *nuper*, and 55, *iam pridem*). The younger man compliments him ironically and they exchange perhaps significant gifts. See further Lee (1977).

There are two songs in Theocritus *Idyll* VII, the first containing a reference to Daphnis, but they do not match in length or balance in structure; that is an added refinement of Virgil's.

'Does Daphnis stand for a real person?' the reader wonders, raising a tempting question endlessly debated; see notes on 56 ff. and IX.47.

Pope's 'Fourth Pastoral: Winter, or Daphne' is an elegant but mostly lifeless imitation, written in his teens and published in 1709; it has one memorable line:

> The moon, serene in glory, mounts the sky.

ECLOGA V

MENALCAS MOPSVS

Me. Cur non, Mopse, boni quoniam conuenimus ambo,
tu calamos inflare leuis, ego dicere uersus,
hic corylis mixtas inter consedimus ulmos?
Mo. Tu maior; tibi me est aequum parere, Menalca,
siue sub incertas Zephyris motantibus umbras
siue antro potius succedimus. aspice, ut antrum
silvestris raris sparsit labrusca racemis.
Me. Montibus in nostris solus tibi certat Amyntas.
Mo. Quid, si idem certet Phoebum superare canendo?
Me. Incipe, Mopse, prior, si quos aut Phyllidis ignis
aut Alconis habes laudes aut iurgia Codri.
incipe: pascentis seruabit Tityrus haedos.
Mo. Immo haec, in uiridi nuper quae cortice fagi
carmina descripsi et modulans alterna notaui,
experiar: tu deinde iubeto ut certet Amyntas.
Me. Lenta salix quantum pallenti cedit oliuae,
puniceis humilis quantum saliunca rosetis,
iudicio nostro tantum tibi cedit Amyntas.
sed tu desine plura, puer: successimus antro.
Mo. Exstinctum Nymphae crudeli funere Daphnin
flebant (uos coryli testes et flumina Nymphis),
cum complexa sui corpus miserabile nati
atque deos atque astra uocat crudelia mater.
non ulli pastos illis egere diebus
frigida, Daphni, boues ad flumina; nulla neque amnem
libauit quadripes nec graminis attigit herbam.
Daphni, tuum Poenos etiam ingemuisse leones
interitum montesque feri siluaeque loquuntur.
Daphnis et Armenias curru subiungere tigris
instituit, Daphnis thiasos inducere Bacchi
et foliis lentas intexere mollibus hastas.
uitis ut arboribus decori est, ut uitibus uuae,
ut gregibus tauri, segetes ut pinguibus aruis,

ECLOGUE V

MENALCAS MOPSUS

Me. Why don't we, Mopsus, meeting like this, good men both,
You to blow the light reeds, I to versify,
Sit down together here where hazels mix with elms?
Mo. You're senior, Menalcas; I owe you deference,
Whether we go where fitful Zephyrs make uncertain
Shade, or into the cave instead. See how the cave
Is dappled by a woodland vine's rare grape-clusters.
Me. Only Amyntas in our hills competes with you.
Mo. What? He might just as well compete to outplay Phoebus.
Me. Then, Mopsus, you start first – with Phyllis' flames perhaps
Or Alcon's praises or a flyting against Codrus.
You start, and Tityrus will watch the grazing kids.
Mo. No, I'll try out the song I wrote down recently
On green beech bark, noting the tune between the lines:
Then you can tell Amyntas to compete with me.
Me. As surely as tough willow yields to the pale olive,
Or humble red valerian to the crimson rose,
So does Amyntas in our judgement yield to you.
But no more talk, lad: we have come into the cave.
Mo. The Nymphs for Daphnis, cut off by a cruel death,
Shed tears (you streams and hazels witness for the Nymphs),
When, clasping her own son's poor body in her arms,
A mother called both gods and stars alike cruel.
In those days there were none who drove their pastured cattle
To the cool rivers, Daphnis; no four-footed beast
Would either lap the stream or touch a blade of grass.
The wild hills, Daphnis, and the forests even tell
How Punic lions roared in grief at your destruction.
Daphnis ordained to yoke Armenian tigresses
To chariots, Daphnis to lead on the Bacchic rout
And twine tough javelins with gentle foliage.
As vines are glorious for trees, as grapes for vines,
As bulls for herds, and standing crops for fertile fields,

tu decus omne tuis. postquam te fata tulerunt,
ipsa Pales agros atque ipse reliquit Apollo.
grandia saepe quibus mandauimus hordea sulcis,
infelix lolium et steriles nascuntur auenae;
pro molli uiola, pro purpureo narcisso
carduus et spinis surgit paliurus acutis.
spargite humum foliis, inducite fontibus umbras,
pastores (mandat fieri sibi talia Daphnis),
et tumulum facite, et tumulo superaddite carmen:
'Daphnis ego in siluis, hinc usque ad sidera notus,
formosi pecoris custos, formosior ipse.'

Me. Tale tuum carmen nobis, diuine poeta,
quale sopor fessis in gramine, quale per aestum
dulcis aquae saliente sitim restinguere riuo.
nec calamis solum aequiperas, sed uoce magistrum:
fortunate puer, tu nunc eris alter ab illo.
nos tamen haec quocumque modo tibi nostra uicissim
dicemus, Daphninque tuum tollemus ad astra;
Daphnin ad astra feremus: amauit nos quoque Daphnis.

Mo. An quicquam nobis tali sit munere maius?
et puer ipse fuit cantari dignus, et ista
iam pridem Stimichon laudauit carmina nobis.

Me. Candidus insuetum miratur limen Olympi
sub pedibusque uidet nubes et sidera Daphnis.
ergo alacris siluas et cetera rura uoluptas
Panaque pastoresque tenet Dryadasque puellas.
nec lupus insidias pecori, nec retia ceruis
ulla dolum meditantur: amat bonus otia Daphnis.
ipsi laetitia uoces ad sidera iactant
intonsi montes; ipsae iam carmina rupes,
ipsa sonant arbusta: 'deus, deus ille, Menalca!'
sis bonus o felixque tuis! en quattuor aras:
ecce duas tibi, Daphni, duas altaria Phoebo.
pocula bina nouo spumantia lacte quotannis
craterasque duo statuam tibi pinguis oliui,

You are all glory to your folk. But since fate took you,
Apollo's self and Pales' self have left the land.
From furrows we have often trusted with large barleys
Are born unlucky darnel and the barren oat.
For the soft violet, for radiant narcissus,
Thistles spring up and paliurus with sharpened spines.
Scatter the ground with petals, cast shade on the springs,
Shepherds, (that such be done for him is Daphnis' will),
And make a mound and add above the mound a song:
Daphnis am I in woodland, known hence far as the stars,
Herd of a handsome flock, myself the handsomer.

Me. For us your song, inspired poet, is like sleep
On meadow grass for the fatigued, or in the heat
Quenching one's thirst from a leaping stream of sweet water.
You equal both your master's piping and his voice.
Lucky lad! From now on you'll be second to him.
Yet we, no matter how, will in return recite
This thing of ours, and praise your Daphnis to the stars –
Yes, to the stars raise Daphnis, for Daphnis loved us too.

Mo. What greater service could you render us than that?
The lad himself deserved singing, and Stimichon
Some time ago spoke highly of your song to us.

Me. Daphnis in white admires Olympus' strange threshold,
And sees the planets and the clouds beneath his feet.
Therefore keen pleasure grips forest and countryside,
Pan also, and the shepherds, and the Dryad maids.
The wolf intends no ambush to the flock, the nets
No trickery to deer: Daphnis the good loves peace.
For gladness even the unshorn mountains fling their voices
Toward the stars; now even the orchards, even the rocks
Echo the song: 'A god, a god is he, Menalcas!'
O bless your folk and prosper them! Here are four altars:
Look, Daphnis, two for you and two high ones for Phoebus.
Two goblets each, frothing with fresh milk, every year
And two large bowls of olive oil I'll set for you;

et multo in primis hilarans conuiuia Baccho
(ante focum, si frigus erit; si messis, in umbra)
uina nouum fundam calathis Ariusia nectar.
cantabunt mihi Damoetas et Lyctius Aegon;
saltantis Satyros imitabitur Alphesiboeus.
haec tibi semper erunt, et cum sollemnia uota
reddemus Nymphis, et cum lustrabimus agros.
dum iuga montis aper, fluuios dum piscis amabit,
dumque thymo pascentur apes, dum rore cicadae,
semper honos nomenque tuum laudesque manebunt.
ut Baccho Cererique, tibi sic uota quotannis
agricolae facient: damnabis tu quoque uotis.
Mo. Quae tibi, quae tali reddam pro carmine dona?
nam neque me tantum uenientis sibilus Austri
nec percussa iuuant fluctu tam litora, nec quae
saxosas inter decurrunt flumina uallis.
Me. Hac te nos fragili donabimus ante cicuta;
haec nos 'formosum Corydon ardebat Alexin',
haec eadem docuit 'cuium pecus? an Meliboei?'
Mo. At tu sume pedum, quod, me cum saepe rogaret,
non tulit Antigenes (et erat tum dignus amari),
formosum paribus nodis atque aere, Menalca.

And best of all, gladdening the feast with Bacchus' store
(In winter, by the hearth; at harvest, in the shade),
I'll pour Ariusian wine, fresh nectar, from big stoups.
Damoetas and the Lyctian Aegon will sing for me;
Alphesiboeus imitate the Satyrs' dance.
These offerings ever shall be yours, both when we pay
The Nymphs our solemn vows and when we purge the fields.
So long as fish love rivers, wild boar mountain heights,
So long as bees eat thyme, and the cicada dew,
Always your honour, name and praises will endure.
As farmers every year to Bacchus and to Ceres,
So they will vow to you; you too will claim their vows.
Mo. What can I give you, what return make for such song?
For neither does the whistling of Auster coming
Sound so pleasant to me, nor beaches beaten by waves,
Nor rivers rushing down the valleys among rocks.
Me. We shall present you first with this frail hemlock pipe.
This taught us 'Corydon burned for beautiful Alexis';
This also taught us 'Whose flock? Meliboeus his?'
Mo. You take the crook, then, which Antígenes failed to get
For all his asking (lovable as then he was),
A handsome thing, with matching knobs and brass,
Menalcas.

ECLOGUE VI

After a statement of his poetic position and a dedication to Varus (see note on line 7) the poet tells how two boys and a Naiad persuaded Silenus (see note on 14) to sing to them, and how he sang of the world's beginning, the Flood, the Golden Age, Prometheus, Hylas, Pasiphaë, Atalanta and Phaëthon's sisters; after which he described how thc Muses gave Gallus (see note on 64 ff.) Hesiod's reed pipe and commissioned him to write a didactic poem; after which he told of Scylla and of Tereus and Philomela, and then we learn that he has in fact been singing a song composed long ago by Apollo on the banks of the Eurotas.

This uniquely magnificent poem is curiously constructed out of allusions to and narrations of poetical subjects that interested Virgil. It is in fact a catalogue poem (perhaps a poem about poems) one of whose stories is expanded into an epyllion (45–60), and into which is inserted a poetical advertisement of a recently published work of Gallus.

There is nothing at all like this in Theocritus. Scholars have imposed various patterns on the compendium of names and references but none of them is entirely satisfactory; for the best discussions see Stewart (1959) and Skutsch (1969), pp. 163–4.

Prima Syracosio dignata est ludere uersu
nostra neque erubuit siluas habitare Thalea.
cum canerem reges et proelia, Cynthius aurem
uellit et admonuit: 'pastorem, Tityre, pinguis
pascere oportet ouis, deductum dicere carmen.'
nunc ego (namque super tibi erunt qui dicere laudes,
Vare, tuas cupiant et tristia condere bella)
agrestem tenui meditabor harundine Musam:
non iniussa cano. si quis tamen haec quoque, si quis
captus amore leget, te nostrae, Vare, myricae,
te nemus omne canet; nec Phoebo gratior ulla est
quam sibi quae Vari praescripsit pagina nomen.

Pergite, Pierides. Chromis et Mnasyllos in antro
Silenum pueri somno uidere iacentem,
inflatum hesterno uenas, ut semper, Iaccho;
serta procul tantum capiti delapsa iacebant
et grauis attrita pendebat cantharus ansa.
adgressi (nam saepe senex spe carminis ambo
luserat) iniciunt ipsis ex uincula sertis.
addit se sociam timidisque superuenit Aegle,
Aegle Naiadum pulcherrima, iamque uidenti
sanguineis frontem moris et tempora pingit.
ille dolum ridens 'quo uincula nectitis?' inquit;
'soluite me, pueri; satis est potuisse uideri.
carmina quae uultis cognoscite; carmina uobis,
huic aliud mercedis erit.' simul incipit ipse.
tum uero in numerum Faunosque ferasque uideres
ludere, tum rigidas motare cacumina quercus;
nec tantum Phoebo gaudet Parnasia rupes,
nec tantum Rhodope miratur et Ismarus Orphea.

Namque canebat uti magnum per inane coacta
semina terrarumque animaeque marisque fuissent
et liquidi simul ignis; ut his ex omnia primis,
omnia et ipse tener mundi concreuerit orbis;
tum durare solum et discludere Nerea ponto

With Syracusan verses our Thaléa first
Thought fit to play, nor blushed to live among the woods.
When I was singing kings and battles, Cynthius pulled
My ear in admonition: 'A shepherd, Tityrus,
Should feed his flock fat, but recite a thin-spun song.'
I now (for you'll have many eager to recite
Your praises, Varus, and compose unhappy wars)
Will meditate the rustic Muse on slender reed.
I sing to order. Yet if any read this too,
If any love-beguiled, Varus, our tamarisks
Will sing of you, each grove of you, nor any page
Please Phoebus more than that headed by Varus' name.
Proceed, Piéridës. Young Chromis and Mnasyllos
Once saw Silenus lying in a cave asleep,
His veins, as ever, swollen with yesterday's Iacchus;
Only, the garlands lay apart, fallen from his head,
And from its well-worn handle a heavy tankard hung.
Attacking (for the old man had often cheated both
With hope of song) they bind him with his own garlands.
Aeglë joins in, arriving as they grow alarmed,
Aeglë of Naiads loveliest, and, now he's looking,
With blood-red mulberries paints his temples and his brow.
The trick amuses him, but 'Why the bonds?' he asks;
'Release me, lads; it is enough to have shown your power.
Now hear the song you want; your payment shall be song,
Hers of another kind.' And with that he begins.
Then truly you could see Fauns and wild animals
Playing in rhythm, then stubborn oaks rocking their crowns.
Not so much joy does Phoebus bring Parnassus' crag,
Nor Orphêus so astonish Rhódopë and Ísmarus.
For he was singing how through a great emptiness
The seeds of earth and breath and sea and liquid fire
Were forced together; how from these first things all else,
All, and the cosmos' tender globe grew of itself;
Then land began to harden and in the deep shut off

coeperit et rerum paulatim sumere formas;
iamque nouum terrae stupeant lucescere solem,
altius atque cadant summotis nubibus imbres,
incipiant siluae cum primum surgere cumque
rara per ignaros errent animalia montis.
hinc lapides Pyrrhae iactos, Saturnia regna,
Caucasiasque refert uolucris furtumque Promethei.
his adiungit, Hylan nautae quo fonte relictum
clamassent, ut litus 'Hyla, Hyla' omne sonaret;
et fortunatam, si numquam armenta fuissent,
Pasiphaen niuei solatur amore iuuenci.
a, uirgo infelix, quae te dementia cepit!
Proetides implerunt falsis mugitibus agros,
at non tam turpis pecudum tamen ulla secuta
concubitus, quamuis collo timuisset aratrum
et saepe in leui quaesisset cornua fronte.
a! uirgo infelix, tu nunc in montibus erras:
ille latus niueum molli fultus hyacintho
ilice sub nigra pallentis ruminat herbas
aut aliquam in magno sequitur grege. 'claudite,
Nymphae,
Dictaeae Nymphae, nemorum iam claudite saltus,
si qua forte ferant oculis sese obuia nostris
errabunda bouis uestigia; forsitan illum
aut herba captum uiridi aut armenta secutum
perducant aliquae stabula ad Gortynia uaccae.'
tum canit Hesperidum miratam mala puellam;
tum Phaëthontiadas musco circumdat amarae
corticis atque solo proceras erigit alnos.
tum canit, errantem Permessi ad flumina Gallum
Aonas in montis ut duxerit una sororum,
utque uiro Phoebi chorus adsurrexerit omnis;
ut Linus haec illi diuino carmine pastor
floribus atque apio crinis ornatus amaro
dixerit: 'hos tibi dant calamos (en accipe) Musae,

Nerêus and gradually assume the shapes of things;
And now the dawn of the new sun amazes earth,
And showers fall from clouds moved higher overhead,
When first the forest trees begin to rise, and when
Rare creatures wander over unfamiliar hills.
Here he recounts the stones by Pyrrha thrown, Saturnian
Kingship, Caucasian eagles and Prometheus' theft;
Adds at what fountain mariners for Hylas lost
Shouted till all the shore re-echoed *Hylas, Hylas*;
And (fortunate if herds of kine had never been)
Consoles Pasíphaë for love of a white steer.
Unlucky maiden, ah, what madness mastered you!
The Proetides with mimic lowing filled the fields,
But yet not one pursued so base an intercourse
With beasts, although she feared the plough's yoke for her neck
And many a time would feel on her smooth brow for horns.
Unlucky maiden, ah, you wander now on mountains,
But he, with snow-white flank pressing soft hyacinth,
Beneath black ilex ruminates the sallow grass,
Or tracks some female in a great herd. 'Close, you Nymphs,
Dictéan Nymphs, now close the clearings in the woods.
Somewhere, perhaps, the wandering hoof-prints of a bull
Will find their own way to our eyes; possibly he,
Attracted by green grass, or following the herd,
Is led on by some cow to Gortyn's cattle-sheds.'
Then sings he the maid who admired Hesperidéan apples;
Then with the moss of bitter bark surrounds and lifts
The Phaëthóntiads from earth as alders tall;
Then sings of Gallus wandering by Permessus' stream,
How one of the Sisters led him to Aonia's mountains,
And how all Phoebus' choir stood up to greet a man;
How Linus there, the shepherd of inspired song,
His locks adorned with flowers and bitter celery,
Told him: 'The Muses give you this reed pipe (there, take it)

Ascraeo quos ante seni, quibus ille solebat
cantando rigidas deducere montibus ornos.
his tibi Grynei nemoris dicatur origo,
ne quis sit lucus quo se plus iactet Apollo.'
  Quid loquar aut Scyllam Nisi, quam fama secuta est
candida succinctam latrantibus inguina monstris
Dulichias uexasse rates et gurgite in alto,
a! timidos nautas canibus lacerasse marinis;
aut ut mutatos Terei narrauerit artus,
quas illi Philomela dapes, quae dona pararit,
quo cursu deserta petiuerit et quibus ante
infelix sua tecta super uolitauerit alis?
omnia, quae Phoebo quondam meditante beatus
audiit Eurotas iussitque ediscere lauros,
ille canit, pulsae referunt ad sidera ualles;
cogere donec ouis stabulis numerumque referre
iussit et inuito processit Vesper Olympo.

Which once they gave the old Ascréan, whose melody
Could draw the stubborn rowans down the mountainside.
Tell you with this the origin of Grynia's grove,
Lest any sacred wood be more Apollo's pride.'
  Why should I speak of Nisus' Scylla, who (so runs
The rumour), white groin girdled round with barking monsters,
Tossed the Dulichian ships and in her deep whirlpool
With sea-hounds, ah, would savage frightened mariners?
Or how he told the tale of Tereûs' limbs transformed,
What feast, what present Philomel prepared for him,
By what route sought the wilderness, and on what wings
Before that swooped unhappy over her own roof?
All, that from Phoebus' meditation, in old days, blest
Eurotas heard and bade his laurels memorize,
He sings (the smitten valleys tell it to the stars),
Till Vesper came to view in a reluctant sky
And bade the flock be folded and their number told.

ECLOGUE VII

The goatherd Meliboeus soliloquizing remembers how he happened to be present at the great singing-match between Corydon and Thyrsis. He then quotes from memory their actual songs (six rounds of matching quatrains) and recalls that Daphnis as judge declared Corydon the winner.

This *Eclogue* is based on pseudo-Theocritus *Idyll* VIII, though there the quatrains are not in hexameters but in elegiac couplets. Scholars argue about why Thyrsis loses. The common reader may feel that despite the very close parallelism of his quatrains with Corydon's, they are less musical and sometimes cruder in content; for the best discussion see Skutsch (1971).

Ambrose Philips imitates this and *Eclogue* III in his 'Sixth Pastoral'; nothing 'namby-pamby' there. Here is a specimen (61–4):

Soft on a cowslip bank my love and I
Together lay; a brook ran murmuring by:
A thousand tender things to me she said;
And I a thousand tender things repaid.

ECLOGA VII

MELIBOEVS

M. Forte sub arguta consederat ilice Daphnis,
compulerantque greges Corydon et Thyrsis in unum,
Thyrsis ouis, Corydon distentas lacte capellas,
ambo florentes aetatibus, Arcades ambo,
et cantare pares et respondere parati.
huc mihi, dum teneras defendo a frigore myrtos,
uir gregis ipse caper deerrauerat; atque ego Daphnin
aspicio. ille ubi me contra uidet, 'ocius' inquit
'huc ades, o Meliboee; caper tibi saluus et haedi;
et, si quid cessare potes, requiesce sub umbra.
huc ipsi potum uenient per prata iuuenci,
hic uiridis tenera praetexit harundine ripas
Mincius, eque sacra resonant examina quercu.'
quid facerem? neque ego Alcippen nec Phyllida habebam
depulsos a lacte domi quae clauderet agnos,
et certamen erat, Corydon cum Thyrside, magnum;
posthabui tamen illorum mea seria ludo.
alternis igitur contendere uersibus ambo
coepere, alternos Musae meminisse uolebant.
hos Corydon, illos referebat in ordine Thyrsis.

C. Nymphae noster amor Libethrides, aut mihi carmen,
quale meo Codro, concedite (proxima Phoebi
uersibus ille facit) aut, si non possumus omnes,
hic arguta sacra pendebit fistula pinu.

T. Pastores, hedera crescentem ornate poetam,
Arcades, inuidia rumpantur ut ilia Codro;
aut, si ultra placitum laudarit, baccare frontem
cingite, ne uati noceat mala lingua futuro.

C. Saetosi caput hoc apri tibi, Delia, paruus
et ramosa Micon uiuacis cornua cerui.
si proprium hoc fuerit, leui de marmore tota
puniceo stabis suras euincta coturno.

T. Sinum lactis et haec te liba, Priape, quotannis

ECLOGUE VII

MELIBOEUS

M. Daphnis was seated once beneath a rustling ilex,
And Corydon and Thyrsis had combined their flocks,
Corydon she-goats milk-distended, Thyrsis ewes,
Both in the flower of their ages, Arcadians both,
Well-paired at singing and prepared to cap a verse.
Here, while I shielded tender myrtles from the cold,
My herd's old man, the he-goat, had wandered off; and then
I notice Daphnis. 'Quick,' he says, at sight of me,
'Come here, Meliboeus, (your he-goat and the kids are safe)
And rest in shade, if you can take time off. The steers
Will find their own way through the meadows here to drink.
Here Mincius fringes his green banks with tender reeds,
And swarms of bees are humming from the sacred oak.'
So what was I to do? I had no Phyllis, no
Alcippë at home to pen the lambs I'd lately weaned,
And a great match was promised – Corydon v. Thyrsis;
However, I postponed my business for their play.
They therefore both began competing in alternate
Verses; the Muses wished alternatives recalled.
These Corydon delivered, Thyrsis those, in turn.

C. Nymphs, our belov'd, Libethrians, either grant me song
Such as you grant my Codrus (he is second best
At verse to Phoebus), or, if we can't all succeed,
Here on the sacred pine shall hang a tuneful pipe.

T. Shepherds, with ivy decorate the rising poet,
Arcadians, so that Codrus burst his guts with envy;
Or, if he praise beyond what pleases, bind my brow
With baccar, lest an ill tongue harm the bard to be.

C. For you this bristling boar's head, Delia, from little
Mico, and the branching antlers of a long-lived stag.
If this good luck be lasting, you shall stand full-length
In smoothest marble, calves enlaced in scarlet boots.

T. A bowl of milk each year, Priapus, and these cakes

exspectare sat est: custos es pauperis horti.
nunc te marmoreum pro tempore fecimus; at tu,
si fetura gregem suppleuerit, aureus esto.
C. Nerine Galatea, thymo mihi dulcior Hyblae,
candidior cycnis, hedera formosior alba,
cum primum pasti repetent praesepia tauri,
si qua tui Corydonis habet te cura, uenito.
T. Immo ego Sardoniis uidear tibi amarior herbis,
horridior rusco, proiecta uilior alga,
si mihi non haec lux toto iam longior anno est.
ite domum pasti, si quis pudor, ite iuuenci.
C. Muscosi fontes et somno mollior herba,
et quae uos rara uiridis tegit arbutus umbra,
solstitium pecori defendite: iam uenit aestas
torrida, iam lento turgent in palmite gemmae.
T. Hic focus et taedae pingues, hic plurimus ignis
semper, et adsidua postes fuligine nigri.
hic tantum Boreae curamus frigora quantum
aut numerum lupus aut torrentia flumina ripas.
C. Stant et iuniperi et castaneae hirsutae,
strata iacent passim sua quaeque sub arbore poma,
omnia nunc rident: at si formosus Alexis
montibus his abeat, uideas et flumina sicca.
T. Aret ager, uitio moriens sitit aëris herba,
Liber pampineas inuidit collibus umbras:
Phyllidis aduentu nostrae nemus omne uirebit,
Iuppiter et laeto descendet plurimus imbri.
C. Populus Alcidae gratissima, uitis Iaccho,
formosae myrtus Veneri, sua laurea Phoebo;
Phyllis amat corylos: illas dum Phyllis amabit,
nec myrtus uincet corylos, nec laurea Phoebi.
T. Fraxinus in siluis pulcherrima, pinus in hortis,
populus in fluuiis, abies in montibus altis:
saepius at si me, Lycida formose, reuisas,
fraxinus in siluis cedat tibi, pinus in hortis.

Are all you need expect; you guard a poor man's patch.
Our present means have made you marble; none the less,
If lambing-time recruit the flock, you shall be gold.

C. Nerínë Galatéa, sweeter than Hyblan thyme,
Whiter to me than swans, more shapely than pale ivy,
Soon as the bulls return from pasture to the byre,
If you have any care for your Corydon, come to him.

T. Nay, you can think me sourer than Sardinia's herb,
Rougher than broom, cheaper than seaweed tossed ashore,
If this day's light's not longer than twelve months to me.
Go home from pasture, shame upon you, bull-calves, go.

C. You mossy springs, and meadow-grass softer than sleep,
And that arbutus green whose rare shade covers you,
Fend off the solstice from the flock: now summer comes
Scorching; now buds are bursting on the tough vine-branch.

T. Here's hearth and pitch-pine billets, here's a roaring fire
Ever alight, and doorposts black with ingrained soot.
We mind the freezing cold of Boreas here no more
Than the wolf numbers, or torrential streams their banks.

C. Still are the junipers, and the prickly Spanish chestnuts;
Beneath each tree her fruit is lying strewn around;
Now everything is laughing: but if fair Alexis
Should leave these hills, you'd even see the streams run dry.

T. Parched fields and thirsty grass, dying of tainted air;
Liber begrudges tendrilled shade to these hillsides:
But when our Phyllis comes, each coppice will be green,
And Jove descend abundantly in merry rain.

C. Dearest the poplar to Alcídes, vines to Bacchus,
Myrtle to lovely Venus, to Phoebus his own bay.
Phyllis loves hazels, and, while those are Phyllis' love,
Hazels will never lose to myrtle, or Phoebus' bay.

T. Fairest the ash in forest, in pleasure-gardens pine,
Poplars by streams, and on high mountains silver fir:
But visit me more often, lovely Lycidas,
And forest ash and garden pine will honour you.

M. Haec memini, et uictum frustra contendere Thyrsin.
ex illo Corydon Corydon est tempore nobis.

M. This I remember, and how Thyrsis lost the match.
For us, from that day, Corydon's been Corydon.

ECLOGUE VIII

After a dedication to Pollio (line 10 makes this identification certain), the more honorific for not mentioning him by name, the poet reports the contrasting songs of two shepherds whose music is as powerful as that of Orpheus. Both songs are dramatic (the character in the first being a man and in the second a woman), both have refrain (adapted from Theocritus, *Idylls* I and II respectively) and both, as printed, comprise ten sections of exactly the same length, though the correspondence in the last three sections is staggered. In fact, the refrain at 28a and 76 should probably be excised, thus making nine sections, each comprising twelve lines arranged in varying groups of 5, 4 and 3, as Skutsch (1969), p. 156, makes clear. See also the note on 62–3 below.

Pastorum Musam Damonis et Alphesiboei,
immemor herbarum quos est mirata iuuenca
certantis, quorum stupefactae carmine lynces,
et mutata suos requierunt flumina cursus,
Damonis Musam dicemus et Alphesiboei.
tu mihi, seu magni superas iam saxa Timaui
siue oram Illyrici legis aequoris – en erit umquam
ille dies, mihi cum liceat tua dicere facta?
en erit ut liceat totum mihi ferre per orbem
ola Sophocleo tua carmina digna coturno?
a te principium, tibi desinam: accipe iussis
carmina coepta tuis, atque hanc sine tempora circum
intra uictricis hederam tibi serpere lauros.
Frigida uix caelo noctis decesserat umbra,
cum ros in tenera pecori gratissimus herba:
incumbens tereti Damon sic coepit oliuae.
D. Nascere praeque diem ueniens age, Lucifer, almum,
coniugis indigno Nysae deceptus amore
dum queror et diuos, quamquam nil testibus illis
profeci, extrema moriens tamen adloquor hora.
incipe Maenalios mecum, mea tibia, uersus.
Maenalus argutumque nemus pinusque loquentis
semper habet, semper pastorum ille audit amores
Panaque, qui primus calamos non passus inertis.
incipe Maenalios mecum, mea tibia, uersus.
Mopso Nysa datur: quid non speremus amantes?
iungentur iam grypes equis, aeuoque sequenti
cum canibus timidi uenient ad pocula dammae.
incipe Maenalios mecum, mea tibia, uersus.
Mopse, nouas incide faces: tibi ducitur uxor.
sparge, marite, nuces: tibi deserit Hesperus Oetam.
incipe Maenalios mecum, mea tibia, uersus.
o digno coniuncta uiro, dum despicis omnis,
dumque tibi est odio mea fistula dumque capellae
hirsutumque supercilium promissaque barba,

Muse of the shepherds Damon and Alphésibóeus,
Rivals, at whom the heifer marvelling forgot
Her pasture, by whose singing lynxes were enthralled
And running rivers, altering their courses, stilled,
We'll tell of Damon's and Alphesiboeus' Muse.
But you who now sail past the rocks of great Timavus
Or coast the Illyrian sea – say, will there ever come
The day when I may be allowed to tell your deeds?
May be allowed to cite your songs throughout the world
As rivalling alone the Sophocléan cothurnus?
You were the starting-point, for you I'll end: accept
The songs begun at your command, and let this ivy
Entwine among the victor's bays around your brow.
Hardly had night's cold shadow disappeared from heaven
(When dew on tender grass is sweetest for the flock),
But leaning on smooth olive Damon thus began:
D. 'Be born, Light-Bringer, leading on life-giving day,
Deceived by sweetheart Nysa's undeserving love
While I lament, and though their witness helped me none,
Yet call upon the gods in this my dying hour.
With me begin Maenalian verses, flute of mine.
The woods of Maenalus are ever musical,
His pines talk; he is ever hearing pastoral loves
And Pan, who first found work for ineffective reeds.
With me begin Maenalian verses, flute of mine.
Nysa weds Mopsus! What may we lovers not expect?
Soon mares will mate with gryphons, and the time will come
When timid hinds go down to drinking-pools with hounds.
With me begin Maenalian verses, flute of mine.
Cut wedding-torches, Mopsus: for you here comes the bride.
Hesper for you leaves Oeta: husband, scatter nuts.
With me begin Maenalian verses, flute of mine.
O what a worthy man you've wed, while you despise
Us all, and while my pan-pipe and my little goats
And shaggy brow and jutting beard are your disgust,

nec curare deum credis mortalia quemquam.
incipe Maenalios mecum, mea tibia, uersus.
saepibus in nostris paruam te roscida mala
(dux ego uester eram) uidi cum matre legentem.
alter ab undecimo tum me iam acceperat annus,
iam fragilis poteram a terra contingere ramos:
ut uidi, ut perii, ut me malus abstulit error!
incipe Maenalios mecum, mea tibia, uersus.
nunc scio quid sit Amor: nudis in cotibus illum
aut Tmaros aut Rhodope aut extremi Garamantes
nec generis nostri puerum nec sanguinis edunt.
incipe Maenalios mecum, mea tibia, uersus.
saeuus Amor docuit natorum sanguine matrem
commaculare manus; crudelis tu quoque, mater.
crudelis mater magis, an puer improbus ille?
improbus ille puer; crudelis tu quoque, mater.
incipe Maenalios mecum, mea tibia, uersus.
nunc et ouis ultro fugiat lupus, aurea durae
mala ferant quercus, narcisso floreat alnus,
pinguia corticibus sudent electra myricae,
certent et cycnis ululae, sit Tityrus Orpheus,
Orpheus in siluis, inter delphinas Arion.
incipe Maenalios mecum, mea tibia, uersus.
omnia uel medium fiat mare. uiuite siluae:
praeceps aërii specula de montis in undas
deferar; extremum hoc munus morientis habeto.
desine Maenalios, iam desine, tibia, uersus.
Haec Damon; uos, quae responderit Alphesiboeus,
dicite, Pierides: non omnia possumus omnes.
A. Effer aquam et molli cinge haec altaria uitta
uerbenasque adole pinguis et mascula tura,
coniugis ut magicis sanos auertere sacris
experiar sensus; nihil hic nisi carmina desunt.
ducite ab urbe domum, mea carmina, ducite Daphnin.
carmina uel caelo possunt deducere lunam,

And you believe no god cares for humanity.
With me begin Maenalian verses, flute of mine.
Inside our fence I saw you, as a little girl
(I was your guide) with mother, picking dewy apples.
I had just entered then upon my thirteenth year,
And could just reach the brittle branches from the ground.
I looked and I was lost. How fantasy misled me!
With me begin Maenalian verses, flute of mine.
I know Love's nature now: on naked hone-stone rocks
Tmaros or Rhódopë or farthest Garamantes
Bring him to birth, no boy of our breed or blood.
With me begin Maenalian verses, flute of mine.
Pitiless Love once taught a mother to pollute
Her hands with blood of sons; you too were cruel, mother.
Who was more cruel, the mother or that wicked boy?
That wicked boy was; yet you too were cruel, mother.
With me begin Maenalian verses, flute of mine.
Let wolves now run away from sheep, let the hard oak
Bear golden apples, let narcissus bloom on alder,
Let tamarisks exude thick amber from their bark,
And owls compete with swans, let Tityrus be Orphêus,
Orpheus in the forest, Arion among dolphins.
With me begin Maenalian verses, flute of mine.
Sink the whole world in ocean. Farewell now the woods:
Down from an airy mountain crag into the waves
I'll dive – a dying man's last gift, for her to keep.
Break off, my flute, break off Maenalian verses now.'
Thus Damon. Alphesiboeus' reply, Pierians,
You must reveal: we cannot all do everything.
A. 'Fetch water and around this altar wind soft wool
And burn the sappy vervain and male frankincense,
For by these magic rituals I hope to turn
My sweetheart's sanity; only spells are lacking now.
Draw Daphnis back from town, my spells, draw Daphnis home.
Spells even have power to draw the moon down from the sky,

carminibus Circe socios mutauit Vlixi,
frigidus in pratis cantando rumpitur anguis.
  ducite ab urbe domum, mea carmina, ducite Daphnin.
terna tibi haec primum triplici diuersa colore
licia circumdo, terque haec altaria circum
effigiem duco; numero deus impare gaudet.
  ducite ab urbe domum, mea carmina, ducite Daphnin.
necte tribus nodis ternos, Amarylli, colores;
necte, Amarylli, modo et 'Veneris' dic 'uincula necto.'
  ducite ab urbe domum, mea carmina, ducite Daphnin
limus ut hic durescit, et haec ut cera liquescit
uno eodemque igni, sic nostro Daphnis amore.
sparge molam et fragilis incende bitumine lauros:
Daphnis me malus urit, ego hanc in Daphnide laurum.
  ducite ab urbe domum, mea carmina, ducite Daphnin.
talis amor Daphnin qualis cum fessa iuuencum
per nemora atque altos quaerendo bucula lucos
propter aquae riuum uiridi procumbit in ulua
perdita, nec serae meminit decedere nocti,
talis amor teneat, nec sit mihi cura mederi.
  ducite ab urbe domum, mea carmina, ducite Daphnin:
has olim exuuias mihi perfidus ille reliquit,
pignora cara sui, quae nunc ego limine in ipso,
Terra, tibi mando; debent haec pignora Daphnin.
  ducite ab urbe domum, mea carmina, ducite Daphnin.
has herbas atque haec Ponto mihi lecta uenena
ipse dedit Moeris (nascuntur plurima Ponto);
his ego saepe lupum fieri et se condere siluis
Moerim, saepe animas imis excire sepulcris,
atque satas alio uidi traducere messis.
  ducite ab urbe domum, mea carmina, ducite Daphnin.
fer cineres, Amarylli, foras riuoque fluenti
transque caput iace, nec respexeris. his ego Daphnin
adgrediar; nihil ille deos, nil carmina curat.
  ducite ab urbe domum, mea carmina, ducite Daphnin.

Circë by spells transformed the shipmates of Ulýsses,
The clammy field-snake splits apart when spells are cast.
Draw Daphnis back from town, my spells, draw Daphnis home.
First with these triple threads in separate colours three
I bind you, then about this altar thrice I bear
Your puppet self; uneven numbers please the god.
Draw Daphnis back from town, my spells, draw Daphnis home.
Tie the three colours, Amaryllis, in three knots;
Just tie them and repeat "The Venus knot I tie."
Draw Daphnis back from town, my spells, draw Daphnis home.
As this wax liquefies and this mud solidifies
In one and the same fire, so Daphnis in our love.
Sprinkle the meal and burn the brittle bay with pitch:
False Daphnis burns me, I burn Daphnis in this bay.
Draw Daphnis back from town, my spells, draw Daphnis home.
Such love as holds the heifer, wearied by the search
Through woodland glades and tall plantations for her steer,
When by a running stream she sinks down in green sedge
Despairing, and forgets at midnight to go home,
Such love hold Daphnis; be its cure no care of mine.
Draw Daphnis back from town, my spells, draw Daphnis home.
These keepsakes in old days the traitor left with me,
Dear pledges of himself, which now here at the door,
Earth, I entrust to you; these pledges owe me Daphnis.
Draw Daphnis back from town, my spells, draw Daphnis home.
These poisons and these herbs gathered for me in Pontus
Moeris himself has given (plenty grow in Pontus);
Moeris with these has turned wolf often and hid himself
In the woods, has often called up ghosts from deepest graves
And spirited (I've seen it) growing crops elsewhere.
Draw Daphnis back from town, my spells, draw Daphnis home.
Take out the ashes, Amaryllis, and throw them into
The stream over your head and don't look back. With these
I'll get at Daphnis; little he cares for gods or spells.
Draw Daphnis back from town, my spells, draw Daphnis home.

'aspice: corripuit tremulis altaria flammis
sponte sua, dum ferre moror, cinis ipse. bonum sit!'
nescio quid certe est, et Hylax in limine latrat.
credimus? an, qui amant, ipsi sibi somnia fingunt?
  parcite, ab urbe uenit, iam parcite carmina, Daphnis.

"Look! On the altar the ash flares up in flickering flame
Spontaneously, before I've touched it. Luck be ours!"
Something's afoot, yes – and Hylax in the doorway barks.
A sure sign? Or do lovers invent their private dreams?
Forbear, my spells, forbear, now Daphnis comes from town.'

ECLOGUE IX

This poem dramatizes the preliminaries to a friendly singing-match that never takes place. Young Lycidas meets old Moeris on his way to town and learns that Moeris's master, the poet Menalcas, has been evicted from his small farm and nearly killed. They proceed to recall snatches of Menalcas's poetry, two translated from Theocritus and two relating to contemporary events. Lycidas is anxious for a singing-match, while admitting that he is no match for two contemporary Roman poets whom he mentions by name, but Moeris pleads forgetfulness and loss of voice. They walk on towards the city, postponing the singing until Menalcas arrives.

Lines 1–16, 27–9 and 50 pair this *Eclogue* with *Eclogue* I; most scholars believe that *Eclogue* I was composed later but put first in the collection to compliment Octavian. See Winterbottom (1976).

William Barnes's 'Eclogue: The Common A-took in' is comparable:

> Good morn t'ye, John. How b'ye? How b'ye?
> Zoo you be gwaïn to market, I do zee.
> Why, you be quite a-lwoaded wi' your geese . . .

ECLOGA IX

LYCIDAS MOERIS

L. Quo te, Moeri, pedes? an, quo uia ducit, in urbem?
M. O Lycida, uiui peruenimus, aduena nostri
(quod numquam ueriti sumus) ut possessor agelli
diceret: 'haec mea sunt; ueteres migrate coloni.'
nunc uicti, tristes, quoniam fors omnia uersat,
hos illi (quod nec uertat bene) mittimus haedos.
L. Certe equidem audieram, qua se subducere colles
incipiunt mollique iugum demittere cliuo,
usque ad aquam et ueteres, iam fracta cacumina, fagos,
omnia carminibus uestrum seruasse Menalcan.
M. Audieras, et fama fuit; sed carmina tantum
nostra ualent, Lycida, tela inter Martia quantum
Chaonias dicunt aquila ueniente columbas.
quod nisi me quacumque nouas incidere lites
ante sinistra caua monuisset ab ilice cornix,
nec tuus hic Moeris nec uiueret ipse Menalcas.
L. Heu, cadit in quemquam tantum scelus? heu, tua nobis
paene simul tecum solacia rapta, Menalca!
quis caneret Nymphas? quis humum florentibus herbis
spargeret aut uiridi fontis induceret umbra?
uel quae sublegi tacitus tibi carmina nuper,
cum te ad delicias ferres Amaryllida nostras?
'Tityre, dum redeo (breuis est uia), pasce capellas,
et potum pastas age, Tityre, et inter agendum
occursare capro (cornu ferit ille) caueto.'
M. Immo haec, quae Varo necdum perfecta canebat:
'Vare, tuum nomen, superet modo Mantua nobis,
Mantua uae miserae nimium uicina Cremonae,
cantantes sublime ferent ad sidera cycni.'
L. Sic tua Cyrneas fugiant examina taxos,
sic cytiso pastae distendant ubera uaccae,
incipe, si quid habes. et me fecere poetam
Pierides, sunt et mihi carmina, me quoque dicunt

ECLOGUE IX

LYCIDAS MOERIS

L. Where do feet lead you, Moeris? Like the road, to town?
M. Oh, Lycidas, we've lived to reach this – that a stranger
(Something we never feared) should seize our little farm
And say: 'This property is mine; old tenants, out!'
Defeated now, sad that the world is Fortune's wheel,
We take these kids (and may they bring bad luck) to him.
L. Surely I'd heard that everything, from where the hills
Begin to drop down, sloping gently from the ridge,
Right to the water and the old beeches' broken crowns –
That all this your Menalcas salvaged with his songs?
M. You had, and so the rumour ran; but songs of ours
Avail among the War-God's weapons, Lycidas,
As much as Chaonian doves, they say, when the eagle comes.
Had not a raven on the left from the hollow ilex
Warned me at all costs to cut short these new disputes,
Your Moeris here would now be dead – Menalcas too.
L. Alas, who'd dream of such a crime? Alas, Menalcas,
Your solace and yourself so nearly snatched from us!
Then, who would sing *The Nymphs*? And who 'scatter the ground
With flowering herbs' or 'cast green shadows on the springs'?
Or there's the song I lately overheard from you,
The day you made your way to our darling Amaryllis:
'Tityrus, till I come (the way's short) feed the goats,
And drive them fed to water, Tityrus, and take care
While driving not to cross the he-goat – that one butts.'
M. Yes, and the song (still incomplete) he made for Varus:
'Varus, your name, if only Mantua be spared
(Ah, Mantua, too near, alas, to poor Cremona!)
Shall be uplifted to the stars by singing swans.'
L. As you would wish your swarms to shun Cyrnéan yews,
And clover-feed to swell the udders of your cows,
Begin, if you've anything. The Picrians have made
Me too a poet; I too have my songs; the shepherds

uatem pastores; sed non ego credulus illis.
nam neque adhuc Vario uideor nec dicere Cinna
digna, sed argutos inter strepere anser olores.
M. Id quidem ago et tacitus, Lycida, mecum ipse uoluto,
si ualeam meminisse; neque est ignobile carmen.
'huc ades, o Galatea; quis est nam ludus in undis?
hic uer purpureum, uarios hic flumina circum
fundit humus flores, hic candida populus antro
imminet et lentae texunt umbracula uites.
huc ades; insani feriant sine litora fluctus.'
L. Quid, quae te pura solum sub nocte canentem
audieram? numeros memini, si uerba tenerem:
'Daphni, quid antiquos signorum suspicis ortus?
ecce Dionaei processit Caesaris astrum,
astrum quo segetes gauderent frugibus et quo
duceret apricis in collibus uua colorem.
insere, Daphni, piros: carpent tua poma nepotes.'
M. Omnia fert aetas, animum quoque. saepe ego longos
cantando puerum memini me condere soles.
nunc oblita mihi tot carmina, uox quoque Moerim
iam fugit ipsa: lupi Moerim uidere priores.
sed tamen ista satis referet tibi saepe Menalcas.
L. Causando nostros in longum ducis amores.
et nunc omne tibi stratum silet aequor, et omnes,
aspice, uentosi ceciderunt murmuris aurae.
hinc adeo media est nobis uia; namque sepulcrum
incipit apparere Bianoris. hic, ubi densas
agricolae stringunt frondes, hic, Moeri, canamus;
hic haedos depone, tamen ueniemus in urbem.
aut si nox pluuiam ne colligat ante ueremur,
cantantes licet usque (minus uia laedet) eamus;
cantantes ut eamus, ego hoc te fasce leuabo.
M. Desine plura, puer, et quod nunc instat agamus;
carmina tum melius, cum uenerit ipse, canemus.

Even call me bard, but I do not believe them.
As yet I cannot rival Varius or Cinna,
But gabble like a gander among articulate swans.

M. I mean to, Lycidas; I'm thinking it out now,
Jogging my memory, for it's a famous song.
'Come here, O Galatéa. What sport is there in water?
Here it is radiant springtime; here by the riverside
Earth pours forth the pied flowers; here the white poplar leans
Over a cave, and limber vines weave tents of shade.
Come here, and leave the crazy waves to beat the beach.'

L. What of that song I heard you sing one cloudless night
Alone? I know the tune, if I could find the words:
'Daphnis, why watch the ancient risings of the Signs?
See where the star of Dionéan Caesar passes,
The star when cornfields should rejoice in crops and when
Grape-clusters on the sunny slopes should colour up.
Graft pear-trees, Daphnis. Grandchildren will pick your fruit.'

M. The years take all, one's wits included. I remember
Often in boyhood singing the long suns asleep.
So many songs I've now forgotten; even his voice
Is failing Moeris now: the wolves saw Moeris first.
Menalcas, though, will sing them for you often enough.

L. You try our love too long with these apologies.
And now the level sea's all hushed for you, and look
How all the airs of the wind's murmuring have dropped.
Here too we're halfway on our journey, for Bianor's
Monument can just be seen. Here, where the farmers
Strip the thick-grown leaves, here, Moeris, let us sing.
Set down the kids here. We shall reach town just the same.
Or, if afraid lest night, before then, turn to rain,
We're free to walk on singing (the road will seem less hard).
I'll take this load of yours, so we can walk and sing.

M. No more of that, lad, and let's do what's urgent now;
Then, when himself has come, the better we'll sing songs.

ECLOGUE X

The eight line introduction is matched (and echoed) by the eight line conclusion, which also serves as a conclusion to the whole *Eclogue* book.

The intervening poem, specially written for Gallus (Virgil's friend and fellow-poet, inventor of Latin love elegy, whom we have already met in *Eclogue* VI), depicts him as dying of unrequited love in Arcadia and visited by three unsympathetic gods, two of whom offer advice. In reply Gallus requests the Arcadians to pipe a song about his love, wishes that he had been an Arcadian himself (for then his love would have been returned), announces that he will adapt his love elegies to the pastoral hexameter, decides to live in the woods, to carve Lycoris's name on trees and to go hunting, then suddenly changes his mind, reflecting that nothing he can do will alter *Amor*, who conquers all and to whom we must submit.

The precise point of this powerful poem remains enigmatic. A possible interpretation is suggested in the notes to lines 3, 6, 31–4, 50–51 and 73. One of the best discussions is Kidd (1964).

Rossetti's 'For a Venetian Pastoral by Giorgione (in the Louvre)' conveys a comparable Arcadian atmosphere, except that Virgil's Arcadians are not 'sad with the whole of pleasure' but glad with it.

Extremum hunc, Arethusa, mihi concede laborem:
pauca meo Gallo, sed quae legat ipsa Lycoris,
carmina sunt dicenda; neget quis carmina Gallo?
sic tibi, cum fluctus subterlabere Sicanos,
Doris amara suam non intermisceat undam.
incipe: sollicitos Galli dicamus amores,
dum tenera attondent simae uirgulta capellae.
non canimus surdis, respondent omnia siluae.
Quae nemora aut qui uos saltus habuere, puellae
Naides, indigno cum Gallus amore peribat?
nam neque Parnasi uobis iuga, nam neque Pindi
ulla moram fecere, neque Aonie Aganippe.
illum etiam lauri, etiam fleuere myricae,
pinifer illum etiam sola sub rupe iacentem
Maenalus et gelidi fleuerunt saxa Lycaei.
stant et oues circum; nostri nec paenitet illas,
nec te paeniteat pecoris, diuine poeta:
et formosus ouis ad flumina pauit Adonis.
uenit et upilio, tardi uenere subulci,
uuidus hiberna uenit de glande Menalcas.
omnes 'unde amor iste' rogant 'tibi?' uenit Apollo:
'Galle, quid insanis?' inquit. 'tua cura Lycoris
perque niues alium perque horrida castra secuta est.'
uenit et agresti capitis Siluanus honore,
florentis ferulas et grandia lilia quassans.
Pan deus Arcadiae uenit, quem uidimus ipsi
sanguineis ebuli bacis minioque rubentem.
'ecquis erit modus?' inquit. 'Amor non talia curat,
nec lacrimis crudelis Amor nec gramina riuis
nec cytiso saturantur apes nec fronde capellae.'
tristis at ille 'tamen cantabitis, Arcades,' inquit
'montibus haec uestris; soli cantare periti
Arcades. o mihi tum quam molliter ossa quiescant,
uestra meos olim si fistula dicat amores!
atque utinam ex uobis unus uestrique fuissem

Permit me, Arethusa, this last desperate task.
For Gallus mine (but may Lycóris read it too)
A brief song must be told; who'd deny Gallus song?
So, when you slide along below Sicanian waves,
May bitter Doris never taint you with her brine.
Begin then: let us tell of Gallus' troubled love,
While snub-nosed she-goats nibble at the tender shoots.
Not to the deaf we sing; the forests answer all.
What woodlands or what rides detained you, Naiad maids,
When Gallus pined away of an unworthy love?
For not the summits of Parnassus, for not Pindus'
Delayed your presence, nor Aonian Aganippë.
The laurels even, even the tamarisks wept for him
Lying beneath a lonely cliff; even Maenalus'
Pine-forests wept for him, and cold Lycaeus' rocks.
And the sheep stand around; they think no shame of us,
Nor be you shamed, inspired poet, by the flock:
Lovely Adonis too fed sheep beside a stream.
The shepherd also came, the heavy swineherds came,
Menalcas came, wet through from steeping winter mast.
All ask him 'Whence that love of yours?' Apollo came;
'Gallus, you're mad!' he cried. 'Lycoris your beloved
Pursues another man through snows and horrid camps.'
Silvanus also came, with rustic honour crowned,
Tossing tall lilies on his head and fennel flowers.
Pan came, Arcadia's god, whom we ourselves have seen
Ruddled with elderberry blood and cinnabar.
'When will it end?' he said. 'Love cares not for such things;
You'll never glut cruel Love with tears, nor grass with streams,
Nor worker-bees with clover, nor she-goats with leaves.'
But sadly he replied: 'Arcadians, will you sing, though,
Of these things to your hills? You are supreme in song,
Arcadians. O how softly then my bones would rest,
If only your reed pipe hereafter told my love!
And how I wish that I'd been one of you, and either

aut custos gregis aut maturae uinitor uuae!
certe siue mihi Phyllis siue esset Amyntas
seu quicumque furor (quid tum, si fuscus Amyntas?
et nigrae uiolae sunt et uaccinia nigra),
mecum inter salices lenta sub uite iaceret;
serta mihi Phyllis legeret, cantaret Amyntas.
hic gelidi fontes, hic mollia prata, Lycori,
hic nemus; hic ipso tecum consumerer aeuo.
nunc insanus amor duri me Martis in armis
tela inter media atque aduersos detinet hostis.
tu procul a patria (nec sit mihi credere tantum)
Alpinas, a! dura niues et frigora Rheni
me sine sola uides. a, te ne frigora laedant!
a, tibi ne teneras glacies secet aspera plantas!
ibo et Chalcidico quae sunt mihi condita uersu
carmina pastoris Siculi modulabor auena.
certum est in siluis inter spelaea ferarum
malle pati tenerisque meos incidere amores
arboribus: crescent illae, crescetis, amores.
interea mixtis lustrabo Maenala Nymphis
aut acris uenabor apros. non me ulla uetabunt
frigora Parthenios canibus circumdare saltus.
iam mihi per rupes uideor lucosque sonantis
ire, libet Partho torquere Cydonia cornu
spicula – tamquam haec sit nostri medicina furoris,
aut deus ille malis hominum mitescere discat.
iam neque Hamadryades rursus nec carmina nobis
ipsa placent; ipsae rursus concedite siluae.
non illum nostri possunt mutare labores,
nec si frigoribus mediis Hebrumque bibamus
Sithoniasque niues hiemis subeamus aquosae,
nec si, cum moriens alta liber aret in ulmo,
Aethiopum uersemus ouis sub sidere Cancri.
omnia uincit Amor: et nos cedamus Amori.'
Haec sat erit, diuae, uestrum cecinisse poetam,

Guarded your flock or harvested the ripened grapes!
For surely, were I mad on Phyllis or Amyntas
Or anyone (what if Amyntas is dark-skinned?
Dark too are violets, and bilberries are dark),
They'd lie with me among willows, under a limber vine;
Phyllis would gather garlands for me, Amyntas sing.
Here, Lycoris, are cool fountains, here soft fields,
Here woodland, here with you I'd be Time's casualty.
But now, demented love detains me under arms
Of callous Mars, amid weapons and opposing foes.
You, far from fatherland, (could I but disbelieve it!)
Gaze – ah, callous – on Alpine snows and frozen Rhine,
Alone, without me. Ah, may the frosts not injure *you*!
Ah, may the rough ice never cut *your* tender feet!
I'll go and tune to the Sicilian shepherd's oat
The songs I put together in Chalcidic verse.
The choice is made – to suffer in the woods among
The wild beasts' dens, and carve my love into the bark
Of tender trees: as they grow, so my love will grow.
But meanwhile with the Nymphs I'll range on Maenala
Or hunt the savage boar. No frosts will hinder me
From drawing coverts on Parthenium with hounds.
Already I see myself explore the sounding rocks
And groves, already long to shoot Cydonian darts
From Parthian horn – as if this remedied our madness,
Or that god learnt from human hardship to grow mild!
Now, once again, we take no joy in Hamadryads,
Nor even in song – again wish even the woods away.
No alteration can our labours make in him,
Not if we drank of Hebrus in the middle frosts
Of watery winter and endured Sithonian snows,
Nor if, when dying bark shrivels on the lofty elm,
Beneath the Crab we herded Ethiopian sheep.
Love conquers all: we also must submit to Love.'
  To have sung of these things, goddesses, while he sat and wove

dum sedet et gracili fiscellam texit hibisco.
Pierides, uos haec facietis maxima Gallo,
Gallo, cuius amor tantum mihi crescit in horas
quantum uere nouo uiridis se subicit alnus.
surgamus: solet esse grauis cantantibus umbra,
iuniperi grauis umbra; nocent et frugibus umbrae.
ite domum saturae, uenit Hesperus, ite capellae.

A frail of slim hibiscus, will suffice your poet.
Pierians, you will make them very great, for Gallus –
Gallus, whose love so grows upon me hour by hour
As the green alder pushes upward in new spring.
Let us arise: for singers heavy is the shade,
Heavy the shade of juniper; and shade harms fruit.
Go, little she-goats, Hesper comes, go home replete.

NOTES

ECLOGUE I

1 'On the appearance of the *Bucolica* one Numitorius replied by writing *Antibucolica*, two pieces (*eclogas*) only . . . the first of which begins: "Tityrus, if your toga's warm, what need of beechen *tegmen?*" '

(Donatus, *Life of Virgil*, 43.)

Toga and *tegmen* are etymologically related; *tegmen* was usually applied to clothes or armour. Lucretius had used *tegmine caeli*, 'sky's covering', and perhaps Virgil is extending that usage.

Tityrus is best pronounced Teety-rus.

2 Milton, *Lycidas*, 66, 'meditate the . . . Muse', and 88, 'But now my Oate proceeds', both come from here.

7 *Deus*: this word was thrown about a good deal in antiquity; so Lucretius calls Epicurus 'a god' and Cicero calls Plato 'that god of ours' and deifies the consul who procured his return from exile.

10 *Agrestis* is used of wild as opposed to cultivated plants, but perhaps 'rustic' is a fairer translation: see *Eclogue* VI.8.

16–17 *Nobis* goes with both *fuisset* and *praedicere*.

De caelo tactus was an archaic religious formula used of anything struck by lightning.

20 *Solemus*: the frequency of this verb here is remarkable (23 *solebam*, 25 *solent*) but clumsy in English.

25 Closer: 'As high as cypresses among bending viburna'.

27 'The indolent': that is, 'me'.

32 *Peculium*: money belonging to someone incapable of legal ownership. A slave could earn money, save it, and hope to buy his freedom.

33–4 Literally: 'Although many a fat victim went out from my pens and ⟨many a fat⟩ cheese was pressed . . .'

38–9 *Vocabant* perhaps because pines and orchards echo Amaryllis's call for Tityrus (an echo represented by the repeated *te* here?), and/or because they need (call for) his attention, weeding, thinning out, pruning, dredging, etc., being necessary.

41–2 Clearly the 'young man' is a *diuus*, and therefore the *deus* of lines 6–7. A contemporary reader would have thought of Octavian (the future Augustus), born in 63 BC and seven years younger than Virgil.

43 Once every month at the monthly sacrifice to the Lares, the guardian spirits of hearth and home.

46–8 Perhaps one should translate *rura* 'the estate', which would be ironical (*facetum*? See introduction p. 12) of a former slave's smallholding. In any case nobody, except perhaps the unfortunate Meliboeus, would covet land as bad as this, however pleasant it might be in the summer.

49 *Feta* means 'with young': either 'pregnant' or 'with a young brood'; here *gravis* ('heavy') makes the choice clear.

54 Shakespeare has 'the *Hibla* bees' at *Julius Caesar* V, i, 34. It was a town in Sicily famous for its honey.

58 Tennyson's 'The moan of doves in immemorial elms' (*Princess*, vii, 206) comes from here – rivulets and bees in that context too make it certain.

62 The Arar is the modern Saône.

The Parthian empire extended from the Euphrates to the Indus.

64 *Nos . . . alii* also suggests 'we others'.

65 The Oaxes is otherwise unknown; perhaps a conflation of the Oxus in Syria and the Araxes in Armenia?

67–9 An awkward passage; other interpretations are possible but less likely.

70 After the battle of Philippi in 42 BC, when Brutus and Cassius were defeated by Antony and Octavian, the veterans in the victors' armies were found land in Italy, mostly confiscated from the supporters of the losing side.

71–2 These lines suggest that Meliboeus is a Roman citizen, of higher status than the freedman Tityrus. The legionary soldier allotted his land is of foreign birth, if we take 'barbarian' literally.

75 It may be argued that I have translated *porrectus* and that *proiectus* is more like 'cast away' (see *Eclogue* VII.42). Certainly it is an unusual word in such a context and suggestive of Meliboeus in exile – typically Virgilian, one might say.

79–81 Tityrus can't offer much; and the bedding has not yet dried out.

81 Literally: 'Soft chestnuts and plenty of pressed milk'.

83 These shadows, though picturesque, sound ominous in the Latin.

ECLOGUE II

2 'Knew he had no hope' goes too far, perhaps. Literally: 'had nothing to hope for, no reason to hope'.

5 *Iactabat*: this imperfect refers to one particular period of time: see *Eclogue* VI.31, *canebat*.

6 *Carmina*: Latin uses the same word for 'song' and 'tune' and the same verb (*canere, cantare*) for singing and playing. Forced to choose in English, one chooses 'tunes' because of lines 31–9.

7 Mynors: *mori me denique cogis?* 'Do you compel me then (*or* in the end) to die?'

12–13 Literally: 'But with myself while I retrace your footsteps/under the burning sun plantations resound to shrill cicadas.'

16 *Niger* 'black', of hair, as in Shakespeare, *Sonnet* 127:
In the ould age blacke was not counted faire,
Or if it weare it bore not beauties name.

21–4 See Theocritus XI.34–8:
A thousand beasts I graze . . .
And from these pressing out the finest milk I drink.
Cheese never fails me, nor in summer nor in autumn,
Not at winter's end . . .
I know to pipe as none of the Cyclôpës here.

21 This is explained by *ouium magistros* ('sheep-masters') in line 33. Corydon is head shepherd on a big ranch in Sicily.

24 This high-sounding line may well be a quotation from some Greek poem. The music of Amphion was fabled to have built the walls of Thebes; he and his brother Zethus were brought up among herdsmen; they killed Dirce, the queen who maltreated their mother. Acte was the old name of Attica, Aracynthus a mountain on the borders of Attica and Boeotia.

25 See Theocritus VI.34–5:
For sure not even my looks are bad as people say.
For lately in the sea I gazed (there was a calm).

28–9 See Theocritus XI.65–6:
Consent along with me to shepherd and to milk
And to set cheese by mixing bitter rennet in.

28 *Sordida* ('dirty') must be quoting Alexis, so *tibi* goes with the adjective as well as with the verb: see 44, *sordent tibi*.

30 Servius's interpretation of this line (perhaps better) is:
'And shepherding a flock of kids to green hibiscus.'

31 Pan was an Arcadian god of shepherds and the wild, son of Hermes, half goat, inventor of pan-pipes.

40–44 See Theocritus III.34–6:
Truly I keep for you a white she-goat with twins,
Which Mermnon's spinning-woman with the dark skin wants.
And I shall give her them, as you're so prudish to me.

42 Literally 'two sheep's-udders a day'.

45–6 Perhaps figuratively – there are lots of water-lilies, or lilies by the riverside. Then Nais could be a girl's name.

51 Usually taken as referring to quinces, but 'the quince is of so austere a taste, that the shepherd could not think of offering it to a young palate' (Martyn).

54 Hence Milton *Lycidas* 1–2:
Yet once more, O ye Laurels, and once more
Ye Myrtles brown . . .

56 Or 'Alexis wants no gifts', that is, he is not mercenary.

57 Literally: 'Nor would Iollas yield if you competed with gifts'. He is presumably the *dominus* of line 2.

58 Auster, the south wind, is the modern sirocco.

60–62 Literally: 'Whom do you flee, ah, madman? Gods too have dwelt in woods,/and Dardanian Paris. Let Pallas care for citadels/which she herself founded . . .' (one thinks of the Acropolis at Athens).

61 Paris was a shepherd when he made his famous judgement between the three goddesses, giving the prize to Aphrodite (Venus), who in return promised him Helen – whence the Trojan war. Dardanus, Paris's ancestor, gives his name to the Dardanelles. Pallas Athene, goddess of wisdom, is called 'saviour of cities' at *Iliad* VI.305.

63–5 See Theocritus X.30–31:
She-goats the clover, wolves the goat pursue,
Sea-gulls the plough, but I am mad on you.

68 Literally: 'for what limit can there be to love?'

69–73 See Theocritus XI.72–6:
O Cyclops, Cyclops, where have your wits flown away?
Maybe you'd have more sense if you would go and weave
Cheese-baskets and cut greenery to bring the lambs.
Milk her that's here. Why chase the one that runs away?
You'll find another Galatea, perhaps even prettier.

70 'Leafy': the elm should be stripped of leaves so that the vine trained up it can get sun.

ECLOGUE III

1–2 *Cuium*: archaic adjectival form of the pronominal genitive *cuius* 'whose'. Donatus in his *Life of Virgil* records this parody by Numitorius:
'Tell me, Damoetas, *cuium pecus* – is that Latin?'
'No, it's Aegonian. That's what they talk in our country.'
Virgil took the idea of this opening from Theocritus IV.1–3 and 13:
Battus. Tell me, O Corydon, whose are the cows? Philondas's?
Corydon. No, Aegon's. He has given them me to graze.
Battus. I suppose you milk them all towards evening on the sly . . .
Poor creatures, what a rotten herdsman they have found.

7 Literally: 'More sparingly are those things, though, to be laid to men's charge, remember'.

8–9 Theocritus V.41–2 is quite explicit about these goings-on; characteristically, Virgil only hints.

20 'Watch your flock': literally 'round up the flock'.

25–7 See Theocritus V.5–6:
What pan-pipe, pray? Have you, Sibyrtas' slave, ever
Possessed a pan-pipe? Why can't you be satisfied,
Like Corydon, with squawking on a pipe of straw?
and Milton, *Lycidas*, 123–4:
And when they list, their lean and flashy songs
Grate on their scrannel Pipes of wretched straw.

32–4 See Theocritus VIII.15–16:
I'll never stake a lamb; my father's difficult –
My mother too. Towards evening they count all the sheep.

37 See Theocritus V.104–5:
I have a pail of cypress wood, I have a bowl,
Work of Praxiteles. I keep them for the girl.
Alcimedon is not otherwise known.

40 This Latin-speaking shepherd with the Greek name knows about Conon and Archimedes, Greek astronomers of the third century BC; the latter's name is metrically impossible in dactylic verse, but he had accurately measured the year and his orrery had been brought to Rome after Marcellus's capture of Syracuse in 211 BC.

46 Orpheus was the legendary Thracian bard whose singing could charm wild animals, trees and even stones, son of the Muse Calliope (see *Eclogue* IV.57).

58 See Theocritus IX.2:
Daphnis, begin the song, and let Menalcas follow.

59 Camenae are the Latin Muses.

60 Damoetas too is a learned shepherd and here alludes to the opening of Aratus *Phainomena* (third century BC):
From Zeus let us begin, whom we men never leave
Unmentioned. Full of Zeus are all the streets,
All human market-places, full the sea
And harbours. Always all of us need Zeus.

68 *Parta*: there is a double meaning, 'obtained' and 'laid', the Latin for 'to lay eggs' being *oua parere*.

70 There is a possible ambiguity in *siluestri*, which could be taken with *puero* as 'Silvester's boy' (literary MSS were written in capitals); *quod potui* could then be taken as apologizing for this weak effort.

70–71 See Theocritus III.10–11:
Look, I'm bringing you ten apples, gathered where
You bade me gather, and I'll bring ten more tomorrow.

79 Mynors punctuates: *longum 'formose. uale, uale,' inquit, 'Iolla'.* taking *longum* with *inquit* ('she says for a long time *or* over a long distance'). Servius takes *longum* with *uale*: 'long be you strong' (the literal meaning of *uale* 'farewell').

80–81 See Theocritus VIII.57–9:
Tempest's a dreadful thing for trees, and drought for streams,
Springes for birds, and flaxen nets for game,
And for a man desire of a young maid.

84 Gaius Asinius Pollio (see *Eclogue* IV.3 and VIII.6–13) was Virgil's patron at this time; his intrusion into the shepherds' world is remarkable and unparalleled in Theocritean pastoral.

85 *Pierides*: the nine Muses, daughters of Pierus, at home on Mount Olympus in Pieria.

88 Literally: 'Who loves you, Pollio, let him come where he is glad you also (are)'. The rather awkward second half of this line may indicate a quotation from Pollio's 'new songs' not quite at home in its new context. 89 may be a quotation from the same source (see *amomum* again in the Pollio *Eclogue*, IV.25).

90 A mysterious glimpse of literary feuds at the time; see also *Eclogue* V.36 note.

102 Literally: 'These certainly (nor is love the cause) hardly cleave to (their) bones'; Donatus tells us that *his* is archaic for *hi*, though it looks like the dative or ablative plural; hence 'them' in the translation.
Mynors prints: *His certe neque amor causa est*: 'For these certainly love is not the cause', taking *neque* as archaic Latin for *non*: see note on *Eclogue* IX.6.

104–7 Riddles here appear for the first time in Pastoral, but the solutions are not agreed. The answers proposed by Servius are unconvincing or incomplete. D. E. W. Wormell has shown that the key to this Alexandrian literary puzzle is 'in what lands'; his answers are (i) at Rome and at Rhodes, where Archimedes' orrery and Posidonius's planetarium were respectively housed; (ii) in Sparta or the Troad, where, according to contradictory traditions, the 'hyacinth' had sprung from the blood of Hyacinthus or Ajax the Homeric *basileus* (king); it was marked with what looked like the letters AI, which were taken as an abbreviation of the name AIAS. For the arguments and evidence see Wormell (1960), pp. 29–32.

ECLOGUE IV

1 Sicilian Muses: the Muses of Pastoral poetry, because Theocritus, inventor of the genre, was by birth a Syracusan.

3 The consul turns out (see lines 11–12) to be Gaius Asinius Pollio, consul in 40 BC, the year of the signing of the treaty of Brundisium between the contending commanders Octavian, Antony and Lepidus.

4 A reference to the Sibyl of Cumae.

6 The goddess of Justice left the earth in the Bronze Age and became the constellation Parthenos (Virgo); see Aratus, *Phainomena*, 96ff.
Saturn ruled during the Golden Age.

8–10 Literally: 'Only, chaste Lucina, do you favour the boy being born, in whose boyhood (*quo puero*) the iron ⟨race⟩ will cease for the first time and a golden race arise in the whole world.'

8 It is simplest to take this of the boy that Virgil hoped would be born to Antony and Octavian's sister Octavia, whose marriage was a condition of the treaty of Brundisium.

10 Lucina, the Roman goddess of child-birth, was identified by some with Diana, Apollo's sister. Apollo was patron god of the Julian clan.

11–12 Literally: 'And with you, moreover, with you as consul this glory of time will come in, Pollio, and the great months will begin to move forward.'

13 'Our sin' presumably refers to the Civil Wars, but may also remind the reader that Rome was founded on fratricide, for Romulus murdered his brother Remus.

17 *Patriis uirtutibus* can be taken with *reget* and/or *pacatum*.

19–20 *Baccar* or *baccaris* is possibly cyclamen, or foxglove; *colocasia* the Egyptian bean.

25 *Amomum*: said to be cardamom.

31 This probably refers to the human wickedness that eventually drove Justice from the earth; see note on line 6.

32 Thetis, the Nereid, stands for her element the sea.

34 Tiphys was steersman of the Argo, in which Jason and his Argonauts sailed to Colchis to steal the Golden Fleece.

36 Achilles, son of Peleus and Thetis, is the central figure in the *Iliad* of Homer.

41 'His team': literally 'the bulls'.

42–5 Pliny, *Natural History*, VIII.191 mentions fleeces of various colours, including red and yellow.
'The books of the Etruscans record a tradition that if this animal (the ram) is covered with an unusual colour it means good luck in everything for the *Imperator*,' (Macrobius, *Saturnalia*, III.7.2).

46–7 An allusion to the refrain of the Song of the Fates (*Parcae*) at the wedding of Peleus and Thetis (Catullus 64.327):
Speed on, spindles, drawing the weft, speed on.

49 Antony claimed descent from Hercules, son of Jupiter; Antony's mother was a Julia and the Julian clan claimed descent from Venus; his bride Octavia was a Julian by adoption.

56–8 For Orpheus and Pan see notes on *Eclogues* III.46 and II.31. Linus was another legendary bard, Orpheus's teacher according to some; see also note on *Eclogue* VI.67.

59 This time *etiam* could be taken with *Arcadia*, as Dr John Van Sickle maintains: 'even with Arcady . . .'

60–62 Strictly *risus* is 'laugh' (there is no noun for 'smile' in Latin), and *risu* can mean either 'with a laugh' or 'by ⟨her⟩ laugh'. Apart from this ambiguity the passage is a famous crux because of the variant reading in 62: *cui non risere parentes* 'him for whom parents have not laughed' (offered by all Virgilian MSS). The reading in the text is derived from Quintilian IX.3.8, who quotes it as an example of a figure of speech – plural (*qui*) followed by singular (*hunc*); being the odder of the two readings it is more likely to have been regularized into the other.

63 Jupiter thought Hercules worthy of his table, Venus thought Anchises (father of Aeneas and ancestor of the Julian clan) worthy of her bed.

ECLOGUE V

2 The infinitives *inflare* and *dicere* are usually taken with *boni*, but they could be governed by *conuenimus*; the translation represents the ambiguity.

5–6 Literally: 'Whether under shade uncertain with Zephyrs that keep moving (it) or rather into the cave we proceed'.

9 Literally: 'What if the same were to compete to overcome Phoebus at playing/singing?'

14 *Modulans alterna notaui*: obscure and not helped by the ambiguity of *carmen* (see note on *Eclogue* II.6). Perhaps 'playing it (the tune) I noted it down alternately'.

17 Literally: 'As lowly saliunca to crimson rose-beds'.
"The *Saliunca* is a plant not certainly known at present,' writes Martyn in 1749, and I believe this is still true.

19 Literally: 'But cease you more, boy'.

20 The legendary Daphnis, son of the god Hermes and a Sicilian Nymph, was born in a sacred grove of bay-trees, whence his name (*daphne* is Greek for 'bay'). Brought up as a shepherd, he was famous for his music and good looks, but died young through the jealousy of a Nymph who loved him. Theocritus sings the sufferings of Daphnis in *Idyll* I.

23 *Atque . . . atque* for 'both . . . and' first occurs here and is a pleonastic rarity.

27 Strictly 'even' goes with 'Punic lions'.

32–4 See Theocritus VIII.79–80:
Acorns adorn the oak, and apples the apple tree,
Her calf the cow, and cows themselves the cowherd.

35 Pales: a Latin divinity of flocks and herds.
Apollo: Nomios, god of pasturage (Servius). Why not simply as sun-god?

36 *Hordea*: according to Servius (on *Georgics* I.210) Bavius and Maevius (see *Eclogue* III.90) attacked Virgil for using the plural of a collective singular noun (as who should say 'salmons' or 'vermins'), producing the line *hordea qui dixit superest ut tritica dicat* '*Barleys* he says; he'll soon be saying *Wheats*!'.

39 *Paliurus* is Christ's-thorn, but this would be anachronistic.

40 *Foliis* can mean 'leaves' or 'petals'; the allusion to this line at *Eclogue* IX.19–20 decides the question.

43–4 See Theocritus I.120–21:
'I am that Daphnis, look, who herded the cows here,
Daphnis who brought the bulls and calves to water here.'

45–7 See Theocritus I.7–8:
Sweeter thy song, O shepherd, than the water yonder
Pours down, down-plashing, from the rock on high.

55 Presumably Stimichon is the master referred to in line 48.

56ff. Virgil's contemporaries could hardly have read of Daphnis's death and deification without being reminded of Julius Caesar, who was murdered in 44 BC, whose star appeared at his funeral games in that year and who was deified in 42 BC.

61 *Otia* is translated 'leisure' at *Eclogue* I.6, its only other occurrence in the *Eclogues*.

64 See Lucretius V.8 (of Epicurus):
A god was he, a god, renownèd Memmius.

67–8 See Theocritus V.53–4:
And for the Nymphs I'll set a great bowl of white milk,
I'll also set another of sweet olive-oil.

80 *Damnabis ... uotis*: roughly 'you will doom to vows' (though *uotis* is ablative), that is, you will compel them to pay their vows by granting their requests.

82 One must be honest here; *sibilus* is 'whistle', not 'whisper' (= *susurrus*) and Auster is not a pleasant wind (see *Eclogue* II.58 and Horace *Odes* III.27.21–2: 'May the wives and children of enemies/Feel the blind movement of Auster rising'). Presumably Mopsus's praise is meant to be double-edged. 'Whistling' scans as three syllables here.

86–7 Surprisingly Menalcas here appears as Virgil's mask, quoting from the first lines of *Eclogues* II and III.

88–9 See Theocritus VII.128–9:

. . . He gave me, sweetly laughing as before,
His throwing-stick, to mark our friendship in the Muses.

90 Probably an intentionally uncomfortable, not to say ludicrous, line. We are now half-way through the collection and Wendell Clausen has pointed out how this first half ends, as it begins, with the vocative of a name which Virgil uses as a mask (for Tityrus as that see *Eclogue* VI.4).

ECLOGUE VI

1 *Syracosio* ... *uersu*: the dactylic hexameter of Theocritus; see note on *Eclogue* IV.1.
Ludere with the ablative can mean 'to play at, with, *or* in'.
Virgil here claims the honour of being the first to write Pastoral in Latin and simultaneously says that the first poetry he wrote was Pastoral.

2 Thalia was the Muse of comic verse; the two spellings are alternative Latinizations of the Greek *Thaleia*.

3–5 Virgil here parallels a famous passage from Callimachus's *Aitia*, Fragment 1.21–4:

When at the very first I placed a writing-tablet
Upon my knees, the Lycian Apollo said to me:
'... poet, feed the sacrifice as fat
As may be, but the Muse, good fellow, slender.'

Since Virgil is here addressed as Tityrus, it was natural that the Tityrus of *Eclogue* I, old man though he is, should have been thought to be Virgil too.

3 *Canerem*: the imperfect could also mean 'intended to sing'.
Cynthius: an epithet of Apollo from Callimachus *Hymn* IV.10, Cynthus being the mountain on Delos where Apollo and Artemis his sister were born.

7 Publius Alfenus Varus was a suffect consul in 39 BC; Servius reports that he won a victory over the Germans. See also note on *Eclogue* IX.27 9.

9 *Non iniussa cano*: the negative can be taken with *iniussa* or with *cano*; in either case he has his orders from Apollo to write pastoral, not epic (which Varus would like him to do).

14 Silenus: an old pot-bellied Satyr, ugly but very wise, tutor and companion of the wine-god Bacchus, of whom Iacchus in the next line is a cult name, here used for wine.

16 *Procul tantum*: difficult. Possibly the line goes:

The garlands, fallen from his head, lay thus-far off.

17 It is not clear where the tankard hung.

34 *Ipse* does not have to mean 'of itself' here; the line could also be translated 'All, and *even* the cosmos' tender globe grew'.

35 Nereus: an aged sea-god, father of the Nereids.

41 Deucalion and Pyrrha survived the Flood and re-peopled the earth by throwing stones over their shoulders.

Saturn's reign was the Golden Age.

Prometheus stole fire from heaven and as punishment was chained to a rock in the Caucasus where an eagle fed upon his liver.

42 *Volucris*: literally, 'flyers, birds'.

43 The boy Hylas went with Hercules on the expedition of the Argonauts (*nautae* here), but fetching water one day was dragged down into the pool by the Water-Nymphs, who had fallen in love with him.

45–6 King Minos of Crete failed to sacrifice a promised bull to Poseidon the sea-god. Poseidon punished him by causing his wife Pasiphae to fall in love with the bull and give birth to the Minotaur.

46 Or '*with* love . . .'

47 *Quae te dementia cepit*: see *Eclogue* II.69.

48 The daughters of Proetus were sent mad by Hera to punish their pride; the goddess made them think they were cows.

56 Dicte was a mountain in Crete, and Gortyn (60) a town there.

61 Atalanta lost her race with Hippomenes by stopping to pick up the golden apples he rolled in front of her. The apples came from the garden of the Hesperides in the far west.

62 Phaethon crashed the chariot of the sun-god his father, set fire to the earth and perished in the flames; his weeping sisters were turned into trees.

64ff. Gaius Cornelius Gallus, friend of Virgil and Pollio, poet and soldier, wrote love elegies and didactic poetry. The Muse here leads him from Permessus stream (a figure for love-elegy) to higher up Mount Helicon, where Hesiod from the village of Ascra in Boeotia (Aonia) had a vision of the Muses and was commissioned by them to sing the truth; he was in fact the first didactic poet.

67 Linus was a legendary Theban poet sage, son of the Muse Urania, who was said to have composed didactic poetry about the creation of the world and the paths of sun and moon (Diogenes Laertius, *Lives of the Philosophers* I.4).

72–3 Probably Gallus had recently published his poem about Apollo's cult-centre at Grynium (Grynia is an alternative form) in Aeolis, Asia Minor; Servius tells us that it was taken from Euphorion, a Greek scholar-poet of the third century BC.

74 Virgil identifies Scylla the sea-monster with Scylla daughter of king Nisus of Megara, who was turned into a sea-bird according to the usual story.

76 Dulichium was a little island near Ithaca under Ulysses' rule.

78–81 Tereus the Thracian violated his wife Philomela's sister and cut out her tongue. Philomela in revenge killed her son Itys and served him up to Tereus at a banquet. Tereus was changed into a hoopoe and Philomela into a nightingale.

83 Eurotas: a river in Sparta where Apollo courted Hyacinthus and accidentally killed him with a discus. We must suppose that he then sang of all the unhappy loves mentioned in this *Eclogue*.

85–6 Literally: 'Until to round up the sheep in the pens and record their number/Vesper bade and came forth in (*or* on *or* from) unwilling Olympus'; or *inuito Olympo* could be ablative absolute: 'against Olympus' will'. Vesper is Hesperus the evening star. Olympus (where the gods live) is probably the sky, by metonymy, rather than the mountain in Macedonia: see *Eclogue* V.56.

ECLOGUE VII

2 Literally: 'had driven their flocks together into one ⟨flock *or* place⟩'. See Theocritus VI.1–2:

Damoetas and the cowherd Daphnis to one place
Had driven the herd together once, Aratus.

3 'Milk-distended' also goes with 'ewes'.

4–5 See Theocritus VIII.3–4:

They both were red-haired, both still boys,
Both skilled to pipe, and both to sing.

Arcadia was Pan's birthplace and sheep country according to Homer. Arcadians were famous for their love of music (Polybius IV.20) and the first settlers on the future site of Rome were Arcadians. But these two 'Arcadians' are near Mantua (see line 13).

13 Mantua, Virgil's home-town, stands on the river Mincio.

19 The Muses were the daughters of Memory (Mnemosyne).

Evidently 'alternative verses' and 'alternatives' here mean 'alternate and matching groups of lines'; see *Eclogue* III.59 where *alterna* refers to answering couplets.

Meminisse could be either a true infinitive 'to remember' or a verbal noun 'the remembering'.

21 *Libethrides*: only here in Latin poetry; it appears in a fragment of Euphorion. These Nymphs had a cave on Mount Helicon, the mountain sacred to the Muses, for whom they stand here.

23–4 Corydon, if defeated, will give up music, dedicating his pipe to Pan, whose sacred tree is the pine.

25 Ivy was Bacchus's plant, the other patron god of poetry.

27 For *baccar* see *Eclogue* IV.19.

29–30 *Paruus* gives the meaning of the Greek name Micon.

31 The meaning 'If this be proper, suitable' may also be present (*facetum*? See introduction p. 12).

33 Priapus was a fertility god with a large phallus.
This hexameter is very unusual in having complete correspondence of metrical ictus and verbal accent (Clausen).

37–8 See Theocritus XI.19–21:
O white Galatea, why cast a lover off,
Whiter than curd to look at, tenderer than lamb,
Friskier than calf, sharper than unripe grapes.
Nerine = Nereid; the original Galatea was a sea-nymph.

41 This plant was like celery according to Pausanias, but deadly, and those who ate it died with a 'sardonic' grin on their faces.

45 Theocritus in V.50–51 had called wool 'softer than sleep'. As sometimes happens, the imitation is a little less apt than the original, for grass is not really as soft as wool.

50 The hut having no chimney, smoke escapes through the doorway.

53–6 See Theocritus VIII.45:
There sheep, there goats bear twins, and there the bees
  Fill the hives full and oaks grow taller
Where handsome Milo walks. But if he goes away,
  Shepherd and pastures then are dry.

61 Alcides: Hercules, grandson of Alcaeus.

70 The second 'Corydon' is 'our champion poet'. Possibly one could translate: 'For us, from that day, it's been Corydon, Corydon'. See Theocritus VIII.92:
And Daphnis from that day was first among the shepherds.

ECLOGUE VIII

2–4 This translation simplifies. Literally: 'at whom, forgetful of grasses, the heifer marvelled/as they competed, by whose song lynxes, enthralled,/ and rivers, changed, rested their courses (runnings)'. Virgil has in mind Calvus, *Fragment* 13: 'The Sun also remembers to rest his everlasting courses', which treats *requiescere* as a transitive verb.

6–13 These lines are addressed to Pollio at the end of his successful campaign against the Parthini in Illyria in 39 BC; he was also famous as a writer of tragedies – hence the reference to Sophocles. The Timavus was a river at the head of the Adriatic.

11 Probably this line refers to *Eclogue* III as the first and *Eclogue* VIII as the last in an earlier collection of *Eclogues* dedicated to Pollio.

17 *Lucifer*: the morning star. (The word's devilish associations for us come

from an old interpretation of Isaiah XIV.12: 'How art thou fallen from heaven, O Lucifer, son of the morning!')

21 Maenalus is Pan's mountain in Arcadia. The refrain is analogous to Theocritus I.64:

Begin, dear Muses, begin a pastoral song.

22 4 Literally: 'Clear-voiced grove and pines talking has Maenalus/always, always he hears shepherds' loves/and Pan, who first suffered not reeds (to be) inactive (*or* unskilled).'

29 30 At a Roman wedding the bride was escorted to the house of the bridegroom by torchlight procession; walnuts were thrown during the ceremony. For Hesperus see note on *Eclogue* VI.86. Oeta was a mountain in Thessaly; Virgil thinks of a line from Catullus's wedding song (62.7): 'For sure the Night-bringer displays Oetéan fires'.

37 40 Based on Theocritus XI.25–8, but with specific alterations and additions that suggest Virgilian autobiography:

Maiden, I fell in love with you when first
You came to gather hyacinths with my mother
Upon the mountain, and I led the way.

38 'Your': plural.

41 Literally: 'When (*or* How) I saw, how I was lost, how a bad mistake carried me away!' *Perii* is ambiguous, used of falling deeply in love and also of being ruined. *Ut* is meant to reproduce the Greek *hos* at Theocritus II.82: 'And when I saw, how I grew mad, how my heart was ravaged by fire!'

43 5 See Theocritus III.15–16:

I know Love now. A grim god. It was a lioness's
Teat he sucked, and in oak-woods his mother reared him.

Tmaros and Rhodope are mountains in Epirus and Thrace, the Garamantes a remote African tribe (*amantes* goes well with Amor!). The spelling *cotibus* (contrast *Aeneid* IV.366 *duris* ... *cautibus*) suggests not only rocks but whetstones (*facetum*?).

47 50 The mother is Medea, who murdered her two boys to revenge herself on Jason when he married another woman.

55 Tityrus is probably the name of the goatherd who supposedly first sang this song.

56 Arion's story is told by Herodotus I.24. A dolphin, attracted by his music, gave him a ride.

58 Literally: 'Let everything become, if you like, mid-sea. Forests, live on' (a formula of farewell).

60 Literally: 'Let her keep this last gift of the dying' *or* 'Let her take this as the dying's last gift'.

62 3 Whereas Damon's song is Virgil's invention (with some Theocritean

adaptations), Alphesiboeus's song is closely modelled on Theocritus II.1–62.

70 A reference to the tenth book of Homer's *Odyssey*. See Milton, *Comus*, 50–53:

Who knows not *Circe*
The daughter of the Sun? Whose charmèd Cup
Whoever tasted, lost his upright shape,
And downward fell into a groveling Swine.

71 The Marsi were said to be able to do this; by tradition this Italian tribe was descended from the son of Circe and Ulysses; there is therefore a hidden connexion with line 70.

85–9 See Lucretius II.355–65:

But the bereaved mother, ranging the green rides,
Looks on the ground for marks printed by cloven feet,
Turning her eyes in all directions, could she only
See her lost offspring anywhere, and standing still
Fills with laments the leafy grove, and many a time
Pierced through by yearning for her steer revisits the byre.
Neither can tender willows and the dew-fresh grass
And those full rivers sliding level with their banks
Delight her spirit and distract the sudden care,
Nor can the sight of other bull-calves in the glad
Pastures divert her spirit and relieve of care.

In Lucretius 'steer' (*iuuencus* 360) refers to a bull-calf, and so it may in Virgil too, for Virgil's *bucula* 'heifer' is later used (by Calpurnius Siculus, *Eclogue* III. 66–7) to refer to a cow with a calf. As often, Virgil is ambiguous where his original is clear.

93 She buries the keepsakes under the threshold (*limen*).

95 Pontus was originally the Greek name for the Black Sea, and used of the lands bordering it; it was associated with Medea, with the poison *aconitum*, and with king Mithridates who by frequent small doses made himself immune.

105–7 Literally: 'Look! The ash itself has caught the altar with trembling flames/ spontaneously while I delay to remove it. Let it be good (luck).'/Certainly there is (*or* it is) something and Hylax on the threshold barks'.

105–6 Spoken by Amaryllis, as *ferre moror*, after line 101, shows, unless one imagines that Amaryllis is the speaker throughout, addressing herself at 77–8 and 101.

107 It is curious that all Virgilian MSS read *Hylas*, of which *Hylax* (Greek 'barker') was a fifteenth-century emendation, accepted by everybody; a good example of the certainty attainable in literary studies, which ignorant fashion nowadays regards as incurably subjective.

ECLOGUE IX

1 See Theocritus VII.21:
Simichidas, where do you footslog at midday
When even the lizard sleeps in the dry-stone wall?

6 *Quod nec uertat bene*: 'which may it nor turn well'; *nec* is archaic for *non*, or *ne* here.

13 This refers to the doves at the ancient oracle of Dodona in Chaonia, a district of Epirus.
Aquila might also suggest the silver eagle carried by every Roman legion.

19 20 These lines refer to lines 20 and 40 of *Eclogue* V, though in fact both are there sung by Mopsus, not Menalcas.

21 2 Literally: 'Or the songs which I picked up from you on the quiet lately,/ when you took yourself ...'

23 5 See Theocritus III.3–5:
Tityrus, my best belovèd, feed the goats
And drive them to the fountain, Tityrus, and the he-goat,
The Libyan yellow, mind he doesn't butt you.
Aulus Gellius in his *Attic Nights* IX.9 criticizes Virgil for using *caper* here, for it normally means a castrated goat.

27 9 Varus (see *Eclogue* VI.7) is said to have been one of three commissioners appointed to distribute land to veterans demobilized after Philippi. Cremona must have supported the losing side, and we gather from *Georgics* II.198–9 (where swans are again mentioned) that Mantua lost land too. Clearly when Virgil wrote this *Eclogue* he still hoped to influence Varus's decision.

30 Kyrnos was the Greek name for Corsica.

32-6 See Theocritus VII.37–41:
For I too am a dry mouth of the Muses, and
All call me best of bards, but I'm not credulous –
No, indeed. In my opinion I can't yet
Outdo Sicelidas from Samos nor Philetas
In song, but rival them as bull-frog the cicadas.

35 Varius, noted for his epic poetry at this time, was soon to become, like Virgil and Horace, a member of Maecenas's circle. Catullus's friend Cinna was famous for his short epic poem *Zmyrna*, on which he spent nine years. A humorously clumsy Latin line, enacting the inferiority?

36 There was a contemporary poet named Anser whom Ovid contrasts with Cinna at *Tristia* II.435.

39 43 See Theocritus XI.42–6 (Polyphemus to Galatea):
But come to me and you will do no worse.
Allow the grey-green sea to thump upon the shore.

You'll pass the night more pleasantly in the cave by me.
Laurels are there, slim cypresses are there,
There is black ivy, there is a sweet-fruited vine . . .

and VII.7–9:

And by the spring
Poplars and elm-trees wove a shady close
With green leaves over-roofing.

42 *Vmbracula*: literally 'sunshades'.

47 A comet appeared in the summer of 44 BC after Caesar's murder and was taken as a sign of his deification.

Dione was mother of Venus, from whom the *gens Iulia* claimed descent via Iulus, son of Aeneas, son of Anchises her mortal husband.

50 The hope for the future expressed here is negated by Meliboeus's allusion to this line at *Eclogue* I.73.

54 'In Italy the sight of wolves is believed to be harmful and temporarily to deprive of speech any man whom they gaze at first' (Pliny, *Natural History* VIII.80).

57–8 See Theocritus II.38:

'Look, silent is the sea, and silent the rough winds'.

59–60 See Theocritus VII.10–11:

We had not yet gone half way nor the tomb
Of Brasilas come into view . . .

60 Servius says that Bianor was another name for the founder of Mantua.

66 See note on *Eclogue* V.19.

ECLOGUE X

1 Arethusa: Nymph of a famous spring near Syracuse, appears here as patroness of pastoral poetry, because Theocritus, its inventor, was by birth a Syracusan.

Extremum: probably has a double meaning: 'last' because this is the last *Eclogue* to be written, and 'most demanding' because the poem is written for a fellow poet.

2 Lycoris is Gallus's pseudonym for his love, the actress Cytheris, a freedwoman and previously Mark Antony's mistress.

Sed quae legat ipsa Lycoris: could also mean 'but for Lycoris herself to read' or even 'but what Lycoris herself reads' i.e. 'the sort of thing she reads' – and she had excellent literary taste if we can trust the recently published Gallus Fragment (see *Journal of Roman Studies* 69 (1979) 138ff.).

3 The line probably implies that Gallus had asked Virgil for a poem.

4–5 The story was that the Arcadian river-god Alpheus fell in love with

Arethusa, who fled from him, was turned into a stream of fresh water by the virgin goddess Diana and flowed from Arcadia under the sea to Syracuse, still pursued by Alpheus.

The Sicani were the original inhabitants of Sicily, named Sicania after them.

Doris, daughter of Oceanus and Tethys and wife of Nereus, here stands for the sea.

5 Mynors prints a comma after *undam* (see *Eclogue* IX.30–32), but to take *sic* after *concede* (see Tibullus II.6.29–30) makes translation easier.

6 Servius tells us that Gallus wrote four books of *Amores*, so the word could here be a reference to that title. This *Eclogue* makes best sense as a celebration of their recent publication in a collected edition.

8 For this conceit see Cicero, *Pro Archia* 19: *saxa atque solitudines uoci respondent*, 'rocks and solitudes answer the voice.'

9–12 See Theocritus I.66–9:

Where were you then, when Daphnis pined? Where were you, Nymphs?
Or down the fair glens of Penéus or of Pindus?
For the great stream you held not of Anapus river
Nor Etna's peak nor Acis' sacred water.

and Milton, *Lycidas*, 50–55:

Where were ye Nymphs when the remorseless deep
Clos'd o're the head of your lov'd *Lycidas*?
For neither were ye playing on the steep,
Where your old *Bards*, the famous *Druids* ly,
Nor on the shaggy top of *Mona* high,
Nor yet where *Deva* spreads her wisard stream.

11 Parnassus: the mountain above Delphi, sacred to Apollo and the Muses, and source of the Castalian spring.

Pindus: a mountain range on the western border of Thessaly, not associated with the Muses, but source of Achelous, eldest of the river-gods and, according to Plato, *Phaedrus* 263d, father of the Nymphs.

12 Aganippe: a spring on Mount Helicon; see *Eclogue* VI.64ff. note.

13–15 Closer: 'Him even laurels, even tamarisks bewailed,/Him, as he lay beneath a lonely crag, even pine-clad/Maenalus bewailed and cold Lycaeus' rocks'.

Maenalus (there is a poetical variant Màenala at line 55) and Lycaeus are Arcadian mountains.

18 Adonis: the young shepherd whom Venus loved and lost when a wild boar gored him.

19–21 See Theocritus I.80–82:

The cowherds came, the shepherds and the goatherds came.
All asked him what his trouble was. Priapus came

And said 'Why waste away, poor Daphnis?'

24 Silvanus: an Italian god of the woods. Apollo and Pan speak but Silvanus simply shakes his head over Gallus.

26 It was not uncommon, especially at festivals, for the gods to be painted red.

31–4 Gallus is made to make his request in the pastoral poem that answers it (see *Eclogue* X.3note); the shepherd's pipe is at this moment telling of Gallus's loves.

31 Arcadians: see *Eclogue* VII.4 note.

37–8 *Certe . . . furor* could also be taken thus: 'Certainly if Phyllis or Amyntas were mine or whatever infatuation . . .'

39 See Theocritus X.29–30:
And the violet is dark and the lettered hyacinth,
But yet in garlands they are gathered first.

40 'They': to cover 'he or she'.

43 That is, I would not have died young as I am dying now of love.

44–5 'Out of a lover's devotion he thinks of himself as being where his girl-friend is, so that *me* equals *my thoughts*' (Servius).

46 *Nec . . . tantum*: either 'only be it not for me to believe', taking *nec* as *ne* (see note on *Eclogue* IX.6), or 'nor be it for me to believe so much'.
At this point Servius remarks: 'These lines are all Gallus's, transferred from his poems.' Exclamatory *a* in three lines running (four, if *a* in 46 be counted – as it could be, for *procul* can take plain ablative) is remarkable and presumably Gallan.

50–51 'Chalcidic verse' is best taken as the elegiac couplet, invented, according to one tradition, by Theocles, who in the eighth century BC led a colony from Chalcis in Euboea to Sicily (see *Etymologicum Magnum* ed. Gaisford 327.5 and Thucydides VI.3). Gallus here says that he will adapt his elegies to the pastoral hexameter ('the Sicilian shepherd's oat'), and in fact this is precisely what Virgil is doing when he quotes from Gallus's *Amores* in this passage (see X.46 note)

52 *Spelaea*: a Greek importation, very rare in Latin and presumably Gallan.

57 Parthenium was a mountain in Arcadia – the Virgin Mountain.

59 Parthians and Cretans (Cydonia was a town in Crete) were famous as archers. Bows could be made of horn; at Homer, *Iliad* IV.105 Pandaros has a bow of ibex horn.

61 Or 'learnt to soften towards human ills', taking *malis* as dative.

62–3 Literally: 'Now neither Hamadryads again nor songs/Themselves can please us; woods yourselves, again depart.'
Hamadryads are wood-nymphs who live as long as the tree together with which they are born.

65–6 Closer: 'Nor if, amid the freezing cold of watery winter,/We drank of

Hebrus and endured Sithonian snows'. Housman on Manilius I.455 so understands the structure. There are two reasons: (i) *frigoribus mediis*, being outside the two *-que* clauses, is common to both; (ii) *Sithonias*, being genuinely geographical like *Parthenios* in 57, not an ornamental epithet like *Partho* and *Cydonia* in 59, does not easily combine with *hiemis aquosae*, which phrase therefore goes with *frigoribus mediis*. Usually line 66 is taken: 'And shoulder the Sithonian snows of watery winter', but this would have to mean 'the snows of the watery Sithonian winter' and the transferred epithet is more complicated than Housman's solution.

65 Hebrus: a river in Thrace.

66 Sithonia: the middle of the three Chalcidic peninsulas, originally part of Thrace.

68 'Beneath the Crab': Latin 'under the star of Cancer'.

69 *Omnia uincit Amor*: perhaps quoted from Gallus, being the second half of an elegiac pentameter.

71 This refers to the *Eclogues* and their 'slender' style; see *Eclogue* VI.5 note. Mynors punctuates *hibisco, Pierides*: again most probably rightly (because of *Ciris* 93–4 *diuae Pierides*), but to take the two words separately is easier for the translator. For the Pierians see note on *Eclogue* III.85.

73 Gallus's love is the collection of poems that describes it, the collection Virgil has just been reading and has found himself admiring more and more; or it is Gallus's poetry in the sense that that is what Gallus loves. The homosexual suggestion is probably *facetum*: see Catullus 50.

76 Why juniper shade is said to be harmful no one knows.

77 For Hesperus see note on *Eclogue* VI.86.

This line is built exactly like *Eclogue* VII.44.

SELECT BIBLIOGRAPHY

Alpers, P. (1979), 'Virgil's Eclogues: Text and Translation', in *The Singer of the Eclogues*, Berkeley, pp. 10–63

Bailey, C. (1947), *T. Lucreti Cari De Rerum Natura Libri Sex*, 3 vols., Oxford

Berg, W. (1974), 'The Bucolics of Virgil (text and translation)', in *Early Virgil*, London, pp. 26–93

Boyle, A. J. (1976), *The Eclogues of Virgil Translated, with Introduction, Notes and Latin Text*, Melbourne

Briggs, W. W. (1981), 'A Bibliography of Virgil's Eclogues (1927–1977)', in H. Temporini and W. Haase (eds.), *Aufstieg und Niedergang der römischen Welt*, II, 31.2, 1267–1357

Camps, W. A. (1969), *An Introduction to Virgil's Aeneid*, Oxford

Clausen, W. V. (1982), 'Theocritus and Virgil', in *The Cambridge History of Classical Literature* II, Cambridge, pp. 301–19

Coleiro, E. (1979), *An Introduction to Vergil's Bucolics with a Critical Edition of the Text*, Amsterdam

Coleman, R. G. G. (1975), 'Vergil's Pastoral Modes', in A. J. Boyle (ed.), *Ancient Pastoral*, Victoria, pp. 58–80

Coleman, R. G. G. (1977), *Vergil: Eclogues*, Cambridge

Conington, J. and Nettleship, H. (1898), *The Works of Virgil with a Commentary* (vol. I *Eclogues and Georgics*), 5th edition revised by F. Haverfield, London. Reprinted Hildesheim, 1963

Currie, H. MacL. (1976), 'The Third Eclogue and the Roman Comic Spirit', *Mnemosyne* 29, pp. 411–20

Curtius, E. R. (1953), *European Literature and the Latin Middle Ages*, translated by W. R. Trask, London

Day Lewis, C. (1963), *The Eclogues of Virgil Translated*, London

Du Quesnay, I. M. Le M. (1976), 'Vergil's Fourth Eclogue', in F. Cairns (ed.), *Papers of the Liverpool Latin Seminar*, Liverpool, pp. 25–99

Du Quesnay, I. M. Le M. (1979), 'From Polyphemus to Corydon', in D. A. West and A. J. Woodman (eds.), *Creative Imitation and Latin Literature*, Cambridge, pp. 35–69

Du Quesnay, I. M. Le M. (1981), 'Vergil's First Eclogue' in F. Cairns (ed.), *Papers of the Liverpool Latin Seminar*, Liverpool, pp. 29–182

Fairclough, H. R. (1935), *Virgil with an English Translation*, Vol. I *Eclogues* etc., revised edition, London (*Loeb Classical Library*)

Gow, A. S. F. (1950), *Theocritus, edited with a translation and commentary*, 2 vols., Cambridge

Gow, A. S. F. (1953), *The Greek Bucolic Poets Translated*, Cambridge. Reprinted by Archon Books, Hamden, Connecticut, 1972

Griffin, J. (1980), 'Greek Literature 300–50 BC' in K. J. Dover (ed.), *Ancient Greek Literature*, Oxford, pp. 134–54

Hubbard, M. (1975), 'The Capture of Silenus', *Proceedings of the Cambridge Philological Society*, New Series 21, pp. 53–62

Kennedy, B. H. (1879), 'Translation of the Eclogues', in *The Works of Virgil with a Commentary and Appendices*, 2nd edition, London, pp. 675–99

Kidd, D. A. (1964), 'Imitation in the Tenth Eclogue', *Bulletin of the Institute of Classical Studies* 11, pp. 54–64

La Cerda, J. L. de (1619), *P. Virgilii Maronis Bucolica et Georgica*, Lyons

Lee, A. G. (1977), 'A reading of Virgil's Fifth Eclogue', *Proceedings of the Cambridge Philological Society*, New Series 23, pp. 62–70

Lindsell, A. (1937), 'Was Theocritus a Botanist?', *Greece and Rome* 17, pp. 78–93

Mackail, J. W. (1889), *The Eclogues ... Translated*, London

Mahaffy, J. P. (1887), *Rambles and Studies in Greece*, 3rd edition, London, pp. 303–8

Martyn, J. (1749), *The Bucolicks, with an English Translation and Notes*, 2nd edition, London

Mynors, R. A. B. (1980), *P. Vergili Maronis opera*, latest issue, Oxford

Nisbet, R. G. M. (1978), 'Virgil's Fourth Eclogue', *Bulletin of the Institute of Classical Studies* 25, pp. 59–78

Page, T. E. (1898), *P. Vergili Maronis Bucolica et Georgica*, London (often reprinted)

Putnam, M. C. J. (1970), *Virgil's pastoral art*, Princeton

Rieu, E. V. (1954), *Virgil: the pastoral poems* (text and translation), London (Penguin Books)

Rose, H. J. (1942), *The Eclogues of Vergil*, Berkeley

Rosenmeyer, T. G. (1969), *The Green Cabinet: Theocritus and the European Pastoral Lyric*, Berkeley

Royds, T. F. (1907), *The Eclogues ... Translated into English Verse*, London (Everyman's Library)

Ruaeus, C. (1675), *P. Virgili Maronis Opera ... ad usum Delphini*, Paris (many later editions and reprints elsewhere)

Rudd, N. (1976), 'Architecture: Theories about Virgil's Eclogues', in *Lines of Enquiry*, Cambridge, 119–44

Servius *In Vergilii Bucolica commentarii*, edited by G. Thilo, Leipzig, 1887

Sisson, C. H. (1974), 'A Reading of Vergil's Eclogues', in *In the Trojan Ditch: Collected Poems and Selected Translations*, Cheadle (Carcanet Press), pp. 193–220

Skutsch, O. (1969), 'Symmetry and sense in the Eclogues', *Harvard Studies in Classical Philology* 73, pp. 153-169

Skutsch, O. (1971), 'The Singing Matches in Virgil and in Theocritus', *Bulletin of the Institute of Classical Studies* 18, pp. 26-9

Snell, B. (1953), 'Arcadia: the Discovery of a Spiritual Landscape', in *The Discovery of the Mind*, English translation by T. G. Rosenmeyer, Oxford, pp. 281-309

Stewart, Z. (1959), 'The Song of Silenus', *Harvard Studies in Classical Philology* 64, pp. 179-205

Valéry, P. (1956), *Traduction en vers des Bucoliques*, Paris

Van Sickle, J. (1978), *The Design of Virgil's Bucolics*, Rome

Wilkinson, L. P. (1969), *The Georgics of Virgil*, Cambridge

Wilkinson, L. P. (1982), *Virgil: the Georgics Translated into English Verse with Introduction and Notes*, London (Penguin Books)

Williams, G. (1968), *Tradition and Originality in Roman Poetry*, Oxford, pp. 303-29 (on the *Eclogues*)

Williams, G. (1974), 'A Version of Pastoral: Virgil, Eclogue 4', in Tony Woodman and David West (eds.), *Quality and Pleasure in Latin Poetry*, Cambridge, pp. 31-46

Williams, R. D. (1979), *Virgil: the Eclogues and Georgics*, New York

Winterbottom, M. (1976), 'Virgil and the confiscations', *Greece and Rome*, New Series 23, pp. 55-9

Wormell, D. E. W. (1960), 'The Riddles in Virgil's Third Eclogue', *Classical Quarterly*, New Series 10, pp. 29-32

Wormell, D. E. W. (1969), 'The Originality of the Eclogues', in D. R. Dudley (ed.) *Virgil*, London, pp. 1-26

DATE